Grandpa

Happy Christmas and Hanukah

with much love, and the hope
of frequent cocktail refreshment

Caleb

THE ART OF
THE COCKTAIL

RYLAND
PETERS
& SMALL
LONDON NEW YORK

THE ART OF
THE COCKTAIL

Ben Reed

photography by William Lingwood

First published in Great Britain
in 2004 by
Ryland Peters & Small
Kirkman House
12–14 Whitfield Street
London W1T 2RP
www.rylandpeters.com

10 9 8 7 6 5 4 3 2 1

Some of the recipes in this book have been
published previously in *Cool Cocktails*,
Martinis and *Margaritas*.

ISBN 1 84172 702 4

A CIP record for this book is
available from the British Library.

Printed in China.

Senior Designer Catherine Griffin
Editor Miriam Hyslop
Production Manager Patricia Harrington
Art Director Gabriella Le Grazie
Publishing Director Alison Starling

Mixologist Ben Reed
Stylist Helen Trent

CONTENTS

THE BASICS   **6**

    Where it all Began   8

    Behind the Bar   14

THE RECIPES   **50**

    Martinis   52

    Power Aperitifs   80

    Margaritas   92

    Champagne Cocktails   102

    Collinses, Rickeys
      and Fizzes   110

    Smashes   116

    Fixes   124

    Sours   130

    Highballs, Coolers
      and Punches   136

    Slammers, Sippers
      and Shooters   146

    Digestifs and Creamy
      Cocktails   156

    Morning After   170

    Mocktails   176

GLOSSARY   **184**

INDEX   **188**

ACKNOWLEDGMENTS   **192**

THE BASICS

WHERE IT ALL BEGAN

The origin of the cocktail is steeped in colourful myth. The term 'cocktail' first appeared in an American dictionary in 1806 as a 'mixed drink of any spirit, bitters and sugar'. Where the word first came from is anyone's guess. Some believe the cocktail was named after an Aztec princess called Xochitl. Others claim it was the innkeeper Betsy Flanagan who first coined the phrase. Betsy, they say, would tie chickens' tail feathers to mugs and cry 'Vive le Cock-tail!' to the French soldiers she was serving. Or does its origins lie in the French *coquetel* meaning mixed drink? Whatever its history, it wasn't until 1920s America that modern cocktail culture really took off.

LIFE AND TIMES OF THE COCKTAIL

Throughout the 20th century the cocktail went through booms and slumps in popularity. It adapted to social phenomena such as Prohibition, war, free love, drug culture, various rises and falls of the stock market and the power of the media, and still flourishes in the 21st century, constantly evolving to suit our thirst for something new and different.

Although many of the cocktails we now regard as 'classic' were invented before the 20th century, it was really the roaring twenties that saw cocktails come into their own. This happy time coincided with a most unhappy state of affairs in the USA – the social experiment called Prohibition (1920–1933). This era had a number of effects on drinking culture. It forced drinkers underground into illicit bars known as speakeasies. These bars weren't dives though – quite the opposite, they were luxurious and lavishly decorated and much more female friendly, which lent additional glamour to cocktails! Because liquor was illegal, inferior bootleg, or moonshine, was drunk, but was often so vile that bartenders would mix it with other juices and cordials to mask its aggressive flavour. The Long Island Iced Tea was created in these times, its seemingly innocuous name designed to fool the authorities. Drinks would also be served in mugs in an effort to distract the hapless police force!

Those bartenders who didn't wish to break the law during Prohibition hotfooted it to Europe or Cuba to ply their trade anew in a different continent, but with as much enthusiasm as ever. This was a particularly creative time for them. Many of the drinks we count as classics today, from the Bloody Mary to the daiquiri, were invented during that period, with the names of the bartenders who created them still hallowed in bars everywhere.

President Franklin D Roosevelt had other ideas about Prohibition and it was repealed in 1933, shortly after he came to office. An accomplished drinker and handy bartender himself, FDR, along with Winston Churchill, was a great protagonist of, among other cocktails, the martini. Indeed, it was during a summit meeting between Joseph Stalin, Churchill and Roosevelt in 1943 that Roosevelt first whipped up Dirty Martinis for his companions.

More should be said about the martini in this opening piece. The most iconic of cocktails, this drink has been enjoyed and tinkered with by a greater alumni of politicians, playwrights and playboys than has ever gathered around a bar. And it was these legendary drinkers who made cocktails the stuff of blurred anecdote and folklore enshrined in times of glamour. Humphrey Bogart's dying words were reported to have been 'I should never have switched from Scotch to martinis' – perhaps not the most encouraging message for non-enthusiasts but a fantastic quote none the less!

Women, never much welcome in saloon bars, were welcomed with open arms to the cocktail lounges of the 1930s. Although there were still laws in some American states prohibiting women from ordering drinks at the bar, this was easily circumvented by implementing table service.

You may imagine that the 1940s bar was a place for reflection and austerity, reflecting the sombre post-war mood. Fortunately, a cocktail can be perfect for times of reflection as well as jubilation. The soldiers returning from the South Pacific to America told tales of the exotic Tiki cocktails made with rum and juices. Such tales prompted a cocktail menu trend that was championed by bartending legend Don the Beachcomber (he was of such high

COCKTAIL MOMENTS

The word 'cocktail' first appeared in print in 1806. It was defined in an early American magazine called *The Balance* as a drink 'composed of spirits of any kind, sugar, water and bitters'.

It was really the early 20th-century Jazz Age that saw the cocktail flourish.

Between 1920 and 1933 Prohibition in the United States caused the cocktail movement to blossom. The Long Island Iced Tea was created during this time – so-called to put the police off the scent.

In 1933 Prohibition was repealed by Franklin D Roosevelt. President Roosevelt mixed the first legal martini in the White House, previously a 'dry' residence. The Dirty Martini (a dry martini with a dash of salty olive brine) is often referred to as the FDR.

American soldiers returning from the South Pacific inspired Tiki cocktail culture during the 1940s. Zombies, Mai Tais and Scorpions were all to become drinks that are synonymous with tropical beaches and 'Hawaiian' shirts!

The 1970s saw the arrival of sweet cocktails like the Tequila Sunrise and the Piña Colada.

Cocktails took a vulgar turn in the 1980s; garish, alcohol- and flavour-heavy cocktails were the norm.

The 1990s were a great decade for cocktails with bartenders being ever more inventive with combinations of flavours and ingredients.

repute that his status was of that usually afforded only to movie stars) and, to a lesser degree, his pupil, Trader Vic. Zombies, Mai Tais and Scorpions were all to become drinks that not only stood the test of time but also remind people of sun-kissed beaches and tropical holidays.

The 1960s were, by and large, something of a non-starter when it came to cocktail consumption. Free love, drug culture and the perceived stuffiness of cocktail lounges meant that cocktails didn't really move forward at all. And so to the next decade . . . Cocktails went the same way that most things went in the 1970s – take your pick from the Tequila Sunrise to the Piña Colada, the seventies did to the cocktail what, well, the seventies did to everything else!

The 1980s didn't help the situation at all, nor did the Thatcher mentality. Spirits (and bank balances) were high but never more so than when it came to the potency of cocktails. For some reason bartenders seemed to do their damnedest to stifle the creativity of cocktail making by performing such demeaning feats as stuffing Mars Bars and jelly beans into bottles of vodka and selling them at irresponsibly cut prices.

The 1990s (my speciality decade) were definitely the years that saved the cocktail, with plenty to celebrate. This was the time when people in London (at least) opted for high-potency, quality cocktails made with premium spirits and fresh exotic fruits and juices. Bartenders started looking more and more towards the kitchen for inspiration and new ingredients. And so it was with the mantle of mixologist newly resurrected, that bartenders did their creative best to prove that anything is mixable. From fresh garlic and Lapsang Souchong tea to liquorice, basil, fennel and even Vimto, the mixologist had a point to prove!

Who knows what lies in store for the cocktail in this new millennium? As long as people keep on ordering mixed drinks, the drinks companies will continue to provide dedicated mixologists with the premium tools of their trade, and as new and exciting spirits are unearthed around the globe, the world is our infinite oyster.

An aspect of cocktail creation that is close to my heart is that cocktails are often more enjoyable when created yourself, whether for a group of friends or just for you after a hard day's graft. One thing I guarantee is that there is a cocktail for everyone and for every occasion; it's just down to you to experiment with some recipes and find it!

PROFESSOR JERRY THOMAS

In the late 19th century pioneers like Professor Jerry Thomas travelled the world spreading the message of mixology. *The Bon Vivant's Companion* written by the professor is a 'must read' for any aspiring cocktail maker.

PROHIBITION

There's no doubt that the Americans are the champions of the cocktail world. Their implementation of Prohibition, perversely, rejuvenated the popularity of the cocktail. American bartenders were driven around the globe in search of new spirits and cocktails while those who chose to remain at home mixed new creations in illicit bars.

BEHIND THE BAR

I can't blame people for thinking that cocktail making is too complex to try at home. The myriad spirits, liqueurs, cordials, syrups, juices, freshly sliced exotic fruit, minerals and other potions that you will see behind a professional bar are an intimidating sight. If you've ever looked up when ordering a drink and observed the bartender pre-chilling, muddling, stirring and straining in pursuit of the perfectly prepared cocktail then you may be forgiven for assuming that it is all just too much hard work to try at home. The reality, however, could not be further from the truth.

HOME BAR ESSENTIALS

In order to run an acceptable bar or cocktail night you need only five bottles of alcohol. Of your five bottles one should be an orange-flavoured curaçao – triple sec would do but I recommend Cointreau. The other bottles should be four of the following: vodka, gin, light rum, aged rum, tequila, bourbon, Scotch or a Cognac. Premium spirits make better cocktails.

In addition to your chosen bottles you will need to prepare some sugar syrup (see page 32). You will also need lemons and limes. Squeeze the juice of ten lemons and ten limes and store in two separate containers, and prepare some to use as a garnish (see page 35).

As you work your way through this book you will come across a great many recipes that you'll be able to make quite easily with these basic ingredients, but don't stop there. There's a whole world of amazing spirits and liqueurs waiting for you, extending as far as South America with classics like the Mojito, margaritas, daiquiris, and the Caipirinha. The beauty of cocktails like the Caipirinha (a Brazilian drink made using cachaça), for example, is that you can substitute vodka for cachaça to create a Caipiroska, or rum to make a Caipirissimo.

There are a number of cocktail recipes that can use different spirits as a base and still taste great. An example of this is the sour – with its formula of sugar and sour with the occasional touch of bitters you can pretty much use any spirit or liqueur as the base in this drink, as long as you are aware of the vague differences of taste and balance the flavour accordingly. Using a non spirit-specific cocktail like this enables you to create a huge array of drinks with the minimum amount of ingredients. When building your drinks cabinet always bear in mind what each new ingredient will bring to the bar.

THE BASICS

STANDARD SPIRITS

Vodka – Smirnoff

London Dry Gin – Gordon's

Light rum – Bacardi or Havana Club
  3-year

Dark rum – Appleton Extra or VS

Gold tequila – Cuervo or Sauza

Scotch whisky – Bell's

Bourbon whiskey – Woodford Reserve

Cognac – Hennessy VS

LUXURY SPIRITS

Vodka – Vox and Stolichnaya

London Dry Gin – Miller's or Bombay
  Sapphire

Dark rum – Appleton Extra or VS

Tequila – Patron Gold, Sauza
  Conmemorativo

Scotch whisky – Johnnie Walker Black

Bourbon whiskey – Knob Creek

Cognac – Courvoisier Exclusif

LIQUEURS

Orange-flavoured liqueur – triple sec,
  Cointreau

Berry-flavoured liqueur – crème de
  framboise, crème de mure, Chambord

Crème de cacao – white and brown

Archer's Peach Schnapps

Cherry brandy

Campari

Cream liqueur – Bailey's

Kahlúa

Amaretto

FORTIFIED WINES

Vermouth – Sweet and dry

JUICES AND MIXERS

Fresh juices – lemon, lime

Other fruit juices – orange,
  cranberry, grapefruit

Sugar syrup

Assorted carbonated mixers – soda
  water, lemonade, tonic water, cola

GARNISHES

Fruit – lemons, limes, oranges

Frostings – sugar, cocoa, salt

VODKA

Vodka can be split into two general categories: Eastern vodkas, which are flavoursome and meant to be sipped and enjoyed on their own, and Western vodkas, which are produced to be imbibed with mixers or as the neutral base in a cocktail.

An argument has raged for hundreds of years as to who invented the spirit – was it the Russians or the Poles? It's an argument that I don't want to go in to. Let us just say a thank you in that general direction for inventing a spirit which, far from being tasteless as many suggest, has as varied a taste spectrum as the next spirit. Anyone who has compared Zubrowka (bison grass-flavoured vodka) with, say, Smirnoff will surely attest to this.

Vodka is mostly made from grain or potatoes but can also be produced using a wide variety of ingredients, including beetroot, carrots or even chocolate! The only criteria for the raw ingredient is that it must contain starch, which can be converted into sugar during the fermentation process.

Eastern vodkas are generally made using the pot distillation method. This method tends to leave behind more impurities (or congeners) in the distillate, which give the resulting spirit its taste. Traditionally, these vodkas were often quite unrefined and herbs and spices were often added to mask the roughness of the spirit. Try Moskovskaya or Okhotnichya for examples of great Eastern vodkas. Vodka is as much a part of the culture in Eastern Europe as a cup of tea is in the UK. It is drunk with appropriate foods, consumed for warmth, and toasted with, but seldom mixed with anything else.

Western vodkas tend to be distilled using the continuous distillation method, which allows for a more refined spirit. These vodkas may be distilled up to four or even five times, as is the case with Vox vodka. Western vodka producers have, in the last decade or so, cottoned on to the idea that there is a place in the market for flavoured vodkas. However, much of the traditionalism and authenticity of the Eastern vodka production is lost in the process of Western production – and the end products stand little comparison with their Eastern counterparts.

As a neutral cocktail base, vodka is a versatile ingredient suitable for any drinking occasion. Try the Vodka Collins for a zingy thirst-quenching vodka cocktail. Explore the many varieties of vodka on the market today, however, and you will eventually be rewarded with one that satisfies both your curiosity and your taste buds with its depth of flavour.

VODKA BASICS

Vodka is mostly made from **GRAIN or POTATOES** but can also be produced using a wide variety of ingredients including beetroot, carrots or even chocolate.

Vodka is as much a part of everyday life in **EASTERN EUROPE** as tea drinking is in Britain. It is drunk with appropriate foods, consumed for warmth, and toasted with – but seldom mixed with anything, as we do in the West.

Vodka gained its popularity in the **WEST** thanks to its reputation as a spirit that leaves no smell on your breath.

There are two methods of vodka production – **POT DISTILLATION** and **CONTINUOUS DISTILLATION**. The former is mostly used in Eastern Europe, the latter in the West.

Vodka is an incredibly **VERSATILE** ingredient and is used in a vast array of cocktails.

GIN

If you want a definition of gin, simply 'predominantly juniper flavoured vodka' would suffice. The spirit has spent a few years in the wilderness, but bartenders are once again embracing gin for its exceptional range of flavours and subtle complexity.

It would be fair to say that gin started its life, as is the case with many spirits, as a medicine. Originally created in Holland by apothecaries in the 1600s, the many herbs and spices known as botanicals added to this grain spirit were thought (correctly) to contain medicinal properties.

While fighting in the Netherlands during the Thirty Years War, British soldiers experienced the gin-induced daring of the Dutch soldiers and coined the phrase 'Dutch courage'. British soldiers began bringing gin back to England with them and distilled the spirit on a small scale. In 1689 William of Orange, a Protestant Dutchman, and his English wife Princess Mary acceded jointly to the British throne and began to encourage the distillation of gin in the UK.

Gin has had its ups and downs over the years. In 18th-century London gin became the object of social hysteria epitomized in Hogarth's painting of 'Gin Lane'. Alcohol consumption had become a serious problem among the poor and gin was named 'Mother's Ruin' as inebriated women were neglecting their children. Historically, gin has been a tipple of not only the working classes but also the ruling classes. The officers aboard Royal Navy ships of the time were given gin mixed with lime juice to battle diseases (whereas the sailors were given a coarse rum as their medicine).

Gin is created by taking a grain spirit and flavouring it with any number of botanicals (but always juniper berries), either by redistilling the raw spirit through these flavourings or by steeping them in the spirit themselves. The range of botanicals can include citrus fruit like grapefruit, lemon and orange; spices such as caraway, fennel and cardamom, ginger and even liquorice. Gin manufacturers often keep the botanicals they use a secret, but recently more and more information is being revealed. Bombay Sapphire, a modern gin partly responsible for making gin fashionable again, actually lists its botanicals on the side of the bottle. This information allows the home or professional bartender a greater insight into what will work well to both mix with and enhance the flavour of their gin cocktail. It is exactly for this reason that bartenders the world over are now rediscovering the joys of a spirit that has long been perceived as stuffy and middle aged. From the Gin Gimlet to the Bramble it would be true to say that gin already plays a huge part in the world of cocktails. Bartenders are continuing to invent new and exciting ways for the drink to reveal its subtle complexities.

GIN BASICS

Gin is created by flavouring a base spirit with various **BOTANICALS** (herbs and spices).

JUNIPER is the predominant botanical in gin. Other botanicals include citrus fruit such as grapefruit and orange, and spices such as caraway, fennel and ginger.

GIN started its life, like many spirits, as a liquid taken to cure an ailment. Combined with the quinine in the original tonic water it made a popular anti-malarial 'medicine' in the tropics.

It was the range of botanicals from the **EAST** that became available through the trade routes that allowed the spirit to be developed.

After banishing gin to the wilderness for a few years, bartenders are once again embracing the spirit for its **EXCEPTIONAL FLAVOUR RANGE** and its versatility in cocktail making.

SINGLE HIGHLAND
MALT SCOTCH WHISKY
TEN YEARS OLD
10
Maker's Mark
KENTUCKY STRAIGHT
BOURBON
OLD STYLE SOUR MASH WHISKY
45% alc./vol.

WHISK(E)Y

A learned friend of mine once said that whiskies are like snowflakes – no two of them are alike. For the Scotsman a whisky will always be malt whisky. Offer an American a whisky and he will ask you what brand of bourbon you have (the USA being one of the countries in the world where brand triumphs over the generic). An Irishman will cherish the lightness of an Irish whiskey and a Canadian will naturally espouse the virtues of his own local spirit.

The production of malt whisky dates back to the 1400s. Monks of the Celtic church distilled *aquavitae* (or *uisge beatha*, in Scots Gaelic) for medicinal purposes. From 1745 onwards whisky spread to the New World with the migration of a large number of Scottish and Irish immigrants. On their arrival in Kentucky they discovered corn (as opposed to the barley and wheat of their homelands), and with their good knowledge of fermentation and distillation a new type of whisky was born.

Although all whisky is made from grain, water and yeast, the four main whisky producing regions of the world all have different methods of production. Add to this the human touch and you begin to understand how each whisky has its own unique character. Scotch whisky falls into two main categories: malt (distilled from barley and aged in oak casks) and blended (malt whisky blended with lighter grain whiskies). American whiskey is made using predominantly corn (US law states it has to have a minimum of 51 per cent but it usually contains more like 80 per cent) with varying proportions of barley and rye added for sweetness and flavour. Another whiskey category, still, is Tennessee whiskey. A popular brand that falls into this style of whiskey is Jack Daniel's, which has slightly different filtration methods (try a Lynchburg Lemonade for a great Jack cocktail). There exists such a diversity of taste and complexity of production within the wonderful world of whisky that it seems strange that the only differentiation on paper between them is the added 'e'.

There is a great deal of experimental fun to be had with whisky of all genres. Where a recipe recommends Scotch whisky, use a light blend to establish a benchmark and then go on to explore the different types of flavours that the various types of whisky will lend to your drink (smoky malts especially!). This process works best in cocktails like the Whisky Sour. There is overlap within the genres too – enjoy the difference between a manhattan and a Rob Roy, for example.

WHISKY BASICS

All whisky is made from GRAIN, WATER and YEAST but the four main whisky producing regions of the world all have different methods of production, creating very different whiskies.

The production of SCOTCH WHISKY dates back to the 1400s when it was first distilled by monks for medicinal purposes.

AMERICAN WHISKEY is made using mainly corn (by law it must have a minimum of 51 per cent) with different proportions of barley and rye adding sweetness and flavour.

Jack Daniel's is a brand of TENNESSEE WHISKEY, which relies on the 'sour mash' process, whereby a little of the previous batch is always used as a 'starter' for the next batch of whiskey.

RUM

Rum has long been one of a bartender's most favoured drinks, either as the base sprit in a mixed drink or served neat. Some even believe that rum will be the new vodka in terms of the world's most popular spirit. There is little doubt that Bacardi is the best-selling brand in the world but it is the sheer number of rum producing countries that lead me to believe that rum has a further reaching influence on drinkers than any other spirit in the world.

When Christopher Columbus visited the Caribbean in 1493 and dropped off some sugar cane to be planted there, it was intended for the production not of rum but of sugar – a highly sought-after commodity in the European courts of the time. In the 1600s, following the British, Dutch and French colonization of the eastern Caribbean islands, rum became a major global industry, especially around Europe and the American colonies.

Rum's history is made even more interesting by its ties to the high seas and piracy. It is the traditional drink of seafarers and the British navy used to hand out a daily ration of a pint of unrefined rum to its sailors. As you can imagine, the ensuing high levels of inebriation proved dangerous so in the 18th century, the ration was mixed with four parts of water. The rum ration was finally abandoned in 1970 on 'Black Tot Day' when mock funerals were held aboard all British navy ships.

Rum is made from the by-products of sugar cane. Usually, a dark brown liquid called molasses is extracted from the cane and fermented and distilled. The liquid is then aged and blended. The key to the production of the range of rum we see today is the different ageing and blending processes. The rum is put into oak barrels for ageing, barrels that have often been used previously for bourbon. As a rule, light rums are aged from between one and three years. The heavier rums are usually aged for at least three years, during which time the interaction of the spirit with the wood and air allows them to mellow. Rum is then blended by the master blender, whose highly specialized job is to ensure consistency of quality and flavour.

Visit Jamaica and you will see rum being sprinkled on newborn babies, poured into the foundations of new houses and rubbed on the chests of the sick – such is the importance of rum to everyday life in the Caribbean, the home of rum. Wherever you go in the world, rum is drunk differently, there are no real rules. I would recommend you try a heavier aged rum (the Jamaican Appleton Extra is a fave of mine) with an ice cube or two or straight up, and a lighter rum (Cuba's Bacardi or Havana Club 3-year) in lighter cocktails like the Mojito.

RUM BASICS

Rum is usually fermented and distilled from MOLASSES, a by-product of sugar cane.

The key to the various rums we know today, which range from 'white' (actually colour-less) through golden colours to dark brown, is the different AGEING and BLENDING processes.

RUM is the base spirit for cocktails like the Mojito, Cuba Libre, Mai Tai, Planter's Punch and various daiquiris.

Rum is considered by some to be the NEW VODKA in terms of the world's most popular cocktail spirit.

Rum is produced wherever sugar can be grown, but the best rum probably comes from the CARIBBEAN.

The sheer number of rum producing countries leads me to believe that rum has a FURTHER REACHING influence on drinkers than any other spirit in the world.

TEQUILA

Tequila has had something of a bad reputation over the years. I read somewhere that if you haven't developed an aversion to tequila after a night on the receiving end before you hit the age of 30 then you haven't really lived! I would certainly agree that if you haven't tasted tequila at some point in your life then you're missing out!

Tequila, made from the juice of the blue agave plant and originally known as *pulque,* has been around in Mexico for centuries and means as much to Mexican culture as vodka does to the Russians. It is recorded in Aztec legend that a lightning bolt split the agave and juice flowed from its heart. Tequila is made in a far more productive way today. The agave is harvested by the *jimadors* (agave harvesters) who cut off its treacherous spikes with their *coa* (a long, sharp hoe-like object). It is then roasted in ovens and crushed before being fermented and distilled at least twice. The resulting spirit is rested in oak barrels, which have often been previously used to age bourbon.

There are four types of tequila as decreed by Mexican law: silver, gold, rested and aged (*plata, joven abocado, reposado* and *añejo* respectively). Silver tequila is aged for less than 60 days in wood and most often served in bars as a shot (the reason for many an aversion!). Gold tequila is a bit cheeky as its colour does not come from ageing, as you would expect, but from the addition of caramel for both colour and flavour. Rested tequila is rested in wood for a minimum of 60 days and a maximum of one year. Aged tequila is left in wood for a minimum of a year but more often, even longer. It is these tequilas that tantalize spirit connoisseurs across the world with their rich complexities.

The most frequently asked question about tequila is 'what will swallowing the worm at the bottom of a bottle of tequila do to me?' The answer is very simple; nothing. Tequila does not contain a worm; it is its sister drink mezcal that will often have the sozzled larva in it. Mezcal is to tequila what brandy is to Cognac; only the spirit created in certain regions of Mexico is allowed to be called tequila, the rest is called mezcal.

Tequila has its fair share of classic cocktails, of which the margarita is the best known (and the most consumed cocktail in the USA.) Some of the best tequila cocktails can be made by replacing the base spirit of other cocktails with the 'agave juice'. Try the Bloody Maria and the Herba Buena and enjoy how the distinctive flavour of tequila cuts through heavier ingredients and makes its mark!

TEQUILA BASICS

Tequila is made from the juice of the AGAVE PLANT, a member of the lily genus not a cactus as commonly believed.

The agave plant can take up to TEN YEARS to mature.

TEQUILA is to mezcal, what Cognac is to brandy (only certain regions of Mexico can legitimately produce the spirit called tequila).

There are four different types of tequila: SILVER, GOLD, RESTED and AGED.

There is no WORM in a bottle of tequila, only in mezcal. The worm is actually the larva of a moth that gestates in the maguey plant (a type of agave).

The worm in a bottle of MEZCAL does not make you hallucinate, although drinking a whole bottle of mezcal to get to it may well do!

BRANDY, LIQUEURS AND FORTIFIED WINES

Brandy, liqueurs and fortified wines all have a significant part to play in the art of cocktail making. Each drink lends its individual flavours and characteristics to the most irresistible concoctions.

Brandy is distilled from wine made from grapes. The most popular brandy to use in cocktails is Cognac, produced in the French region by the same name. Other French regions that both produce and lend their name to brandies are Calvados in Normandy, which produces a dry apple brandy, and Armagnac, a stronger flavoured brandy from the Gascony region. Also very popular in the creation of cocktails are the fruit brandies and eau de vie, which can be made from most fruits. Spain and the United States also produce some very creditable brands. Brandy was once the most popular spirit in cocktails. Today, as classic cocktails are coming back in vogue so, too, is the use of brandy; bartenders are again mixing cocktails such as the Sidecar, the Brandy Alexander and the Stinger.

An ever-increasing number of liqueurs on the market also work to great effect in cocktails. Liqueurs, like many types of alcohol, were originally intended for medicinal consumption and it wasn't until sugar became available to the wealthy in the late 18th century that these drinks were considered suitable for pleasurable drinking.

Liqueurs by definition, although lower in abv (alcohol by volume) than spirits, are sweetened. They have a huge part to play in the balancing and flavouring of cocktails, so don't think for a moment they have a lesser role in your home bar. With an inexhaustible supply of flavours, bartenders see new liqueurs as a constant motivation to stay creative. If you don't believe me try Oh Canada maple liqueur, the Kwai Feh lychee liqueur, The King's Ginger Liqueur or Sour Apple Liqueur and I defy you not to feel tempted to put on your mixological head! Whether herbed and spiced (Chartreuse), fruit flavoured (crème de framboise), creamed (Bailey's), made from flowers (Parfait Amour), seeds or beans (Kahlúa) or tree root (Becherovka), the liqueur corner of your drinks cabinet should always provide the most colour and interest.

Fortified and aromatic wines (wine infused with herbs, alcohol, sugar and water) also have a part to play in cocktail making and the most important of these is vermouth. Martini, Noilly Prat and Cinzano are the brand names you may be familiar with. Without these alcohols, two champions of the cocktail world, the martini and the manhattan would not exist and neither would many cocktails from the last century! Sherry and port are also becoming more and more fashionable mixed in cocktails; once the type of drink that only your granny drank, their popularity has risen so that now drinks like the Port Cobbler and the Sherry Flip appear on bar menus the world over!

BRANDY, LIQUEURS AND FORTIFIED WINES
BRANDY is made in many wine-producing regions around the world but that from France is probably the best.

As cocktails take a slight swing back towards the classic, **BRANDY** has re-emerged as a spirit that bartenders feel comfortable mixing.

Also very popular in the creation of cocktails are the **FRUIT BRANDIES** and **EAU DE VIE**, which can be made from most fruits.

There are an ever-increasing number of **LIQUEURS** on the market. Liqueurs, like many types of alcohol, were originally intended for medicinal rather than pleasurable consumption.

FORTIFIED (and **AROMATIC**) **WINES** also have a part to play in the world of cocktails and the most important of these alcohols is vermouth.

BALANCING FLAVOURS

It might seem, to the untrained eye, that cocktail making is all about throwing the most colourful ingredients into a novelty glass and adding an exotic fruit garnish. In reality, there is far more behind the creation of your average cocktail.

There are two principles that should be applied when creating a new cocktail or recreating an old one (aside from a couple of the classic cocktails which have *carte blanche* to rock the boat as far as I'm concerned). First, the base spirit should provide the bulk of the taste and the addition of sweetening and souring agents should provide the balance. Secondly, if an ingredient cannot be tasted in the drink, don't add it.

If you order a cocktail from a novelty or theme bar (as opposed to a classic bar), you may be served a cocktail that doesn't contain a souring agent – just an assortment of sweet liqueurs and juices. There is a difference between the types of bars that serve cocktails. On the one hand there are those bars that espouse the virtues of fresh produce. Here, you will be served a Screwdriver with freshly squeezed orange juice, or a Long Island Iced Tea with fresh lemon juice. On the other hand are those bars that are more concerned with the sheer volume of drinks going out over the stick, and they usually opt for the cheaper, more efficient options such as pre-mixes (cocktails that are purchased in bulk by the retailer already mixed and packaged, and merely needing the addition of water or alcohol). I don't expect I need to tell you whether we'll be opting to use fresh products or pre-mixes!

If you were to look back through cocktail journals of old, you would notice that most of the drinks mentioned use both a sweetening and a souring agent, often in the form of caster sugar and the juice of a lemon or lime. Although the ratio of one part sour to one part sweet is a good benchmark, your guest will have a personal preference as to whether they prefer their drink sweet or sour, so try to ascertain what their taste buds require.

Let me get one thing clear from the outset though, when we are talking about balancing drinks there is very little you can do when creating drinks with dairy products as the base. Adding a sour will tend to curdle your cocktail. Similarly, balancing drinks containing the unholy trinity of Malibu, Archer's and Midori would require an unnatural amount of sours.

The trick when creating a drink that requires a balance of flavour is to always add less rather than more at the early stages (you can always add more but you can't take it away!). Trying to balance a drink can be equated with trying to

BALANCING BASICS

There is **FAR MORE** to creating a new cocktail than choosing a pretty looking bottle from behind your bar and adding it to your mixture.

The base spirit in your cocktail should always provide the **BULK OF THE FLAVOUR** and the addition of sweetening and souring agents should provide the balance.

If an ingredient can't be **TASTED** in a drink don't use it.

Although the ratio of one part sour to one part sweet is a good benchmark, invariably the drinker will have a **PERSONAL PREFERENCE** as to whether they prefer the drink more sweet or more sour.

Cocktails like cosmopolitans, margaritas daiquiris and the Sidecar are all great examples of **PERFECTLY BALANCED COCKTAILS**, with their formula of base spirit plus almost equal parts of citrus juice and sugar syrup or Cointreau.

Try to make your cocktails using only **FRESH, AUTHENTIC INGREDIENTS**.

balance a dining table with one leg shorter than the other. If you keep shortening one leg at a time you will eventually end up with a coffee table! If you cannot find the correct balance and you have already added large quantities of sweet and sour you will generally end up with a cocktail that lacks the finesse of the drink you are searching for. Cocktails like margaritas, daiquiris or the Sidecar are examples of well-balanced cocktails with their formula of base spirit plus almost equal parts of citrus juice and sugar syrup or Cointreau.

When using the substitution method (substituting the spirit in a tried and tested recipe) for creating new cocktails you will need to consider the flavours of the ingredients that you are adopting. For example, if substituting an aged rum in a daiquiri think about the sweetness of the rum and nip and tuck the recipe accordingly (aged rum will have a more caramel taste so less sugar can be used).

Although you may have a number of liqueurs (which by legal definition have to be sweetened) at your disposal, these not only bring sweetness to your drink but also the flavour of the liqueur itself. If your cocktail needs to be sweetened but not flavoured you will require a neutral sweetening agent, something that imparts no flavour, merely taste.

The principal neutral sweetening agent at a bartender's disposal is sugar. As sugar takes significantly longer to dissolve into alcohol than into water, it is best converted into liquid form prior to adding it to a cocktail. Once converted, the thick, viscous liquid is known as sugar syrup, sirop de gomme, gomme syrup or simple syrup.

As well as adding sweetness to mixed drinks, a dash of sugar syrup enhances the natural flavours in drinks containing fresh fruit. Sugar syrup can also be used to bring substance to a drink that tastes 'thin'.

To make sugar syrup, add a kilogram of caster sugar to a litre of water (or make up smaller quantities as long as you use the same ratio) in a pan and bring slowly to the boil. Stir and dissolve the sugar until the liquid is clear, leave to cool and bottle. It can be kept in the fridge for a good couple of weeks.

It can also be worthwhile using caster sugar for a little bit of added texture (or crunch) at the bottom of the glass. Be aware that if you are shaking a cocktail using caster sugar, you will have to add that little bit more as a large percentage of it will either not dissolve or simply stick to the inside of the shaker. The fun doesn't need to stop there; you could try replacing caster sugar with vanilla sugar or muscovado sugar (in fact experiment with any type of sugar) for entirely different results each time!

To balance against the sweetness of a cocktail, you need to add a sour flavour. Fresh lemon or lime juice is most commonly used, though fresh grapefruit juice also works well (try the pink variety) and certain packaged orange juices work adequately. I'm sure there are other exotic fruits that could be used as souring agents but for sheer availability and cost, I tend to stick to citrus.

SWEET AND SOUR

SUGAR SYRUP is the most commonly used sweetener in cocktails as it is neutral in flavour.

Always have a bottle of sugar syrup handy – not only does this add sweetness when added to a cocktail, it can also STRENGTHEN a cocktail that tastes weak or 'thin'.

Citrus juices (lemon and lime) are the most popular SOURING AGENTS. Try using fresh grapefruit juice for an unusual sour twist.

Avoid using CONCENTRATED citrus juices or cordials as souring agents.

Use a LIQUEUR if you want to add sweetness as well as flavour to your cocktail.

When using freshly squeezed citrus juices, add the HUSKS of the fruit into the mix as well as the juice to add oiliness.

SUGAR dissolves much easier into water than it does into alcohol.

GARNISHES

Garnishes are an essential part of the cocktail. They have not always been treated with respect, however, and for at least a decade those used to dress drinks were garish, over-flamboyant affairs (reflecting the lurid cocktails of the time but not necessarily the flavour of the drink).

These days it is generally accepted that the garnish should add both colour and flavour to a cocktail (in a manner appropriate to the cocktail). So yes, you can dress a Mai Tai with a pineapple slice, cherry and orange wheel as it is a Tiki cocktail (the Tahitian cocktail movement arguably responsible for the cocktail umbrella). But think of putting any of those into a Classic Martini and your bartending days would be numbered!

Lemons, limes and oranges are the three basic cocktail garnishes. Lemons and oranges should be sliced into thin half wheels whereas limes should be cut into wedges. When using limes, you can add more flavour to your cocktail by squeezing and dropping the lime wedges into the drink. Garnishes should always be added to the drink at the final stage of preparation.

Zests and twists are also a great tool in a bartender's arsenal. The lemon twist gently squeezed face down over the surface of the Classic Martini is the perfect example of how the garnish can be the icing on the cake. When taking a twist from a lemon for a martini, always peel the thinnest slice of the peel only, leaving as much of the pith behind on the lemon as possible. The pith is bitter and can offset the balance of a drink as delicate as the martini. A zest tends to be bigger and less delicate than the twist.

For great theatrical effect have a go at the flaming orange zest. Take a thick(ish) zest from an orange and hold it between your thumb and forefinger, skin down, over the drink. Squeeze the zest so the oils pass through a naked flame onto the drink's surface. Your efforts will be rewarded by a flash of light (the oil of citrus fruit is flammable!) and a hint of burnt orange flavour added to your drink (there may also be a slight carbon deposit on the surface – don't worry, it's harmless!). If you're looking for a more ornate garnish try a spiral by peeling off a long rind from a fruit. You can use either a kitchen knife or a canelle knife.

Mint can be used to great effect as a fresh garnish; its fresh clean aroma can even make a huge impact on drinks that aren't mint based. Among the other garnishes at your disposal are all types of tropical or exotic fruit, including strawberries, kiwis and star fruit. When choosing a garnish you should try to reflect some of the ingredients in the drink for the sake of authenticity.

Frostings are also a particularly effective way of adding both flavour and colour to a drink. These include sugar, salt, cocoa powder, grated nutmeg and ground cinnamon. To frost your glass either wipe the rim of the glass with lemon juice or dip the rim into beaten egg white then invert the glass and dip into the powder of your choice, taking care that the powder coats only the outside of the rim and does not interfere with the drink itself.

COCKTAIL UMBRELLA OR FRUIT?
The standard garnishes for cocktails are
LEMONS, LIMES AND ORANGES.

A cocktail umbrella can be an appropriate garnish if used in the correct context. Otherwise, all garnishes should adorn cocktails for the purpose of both AESTHETICS and TASTE. They should be added to the drink only at the final stage of preparation.

The most important thing to bear in mind when you garnish a drink is KEEP IT FRESH!

When taking a TWIST from a fruit, ensure you remove as little pith as possible as this often lends unwanted bitterness to your drink.

Garnish your drink with a THEATRICAL FLAMING ORANGE ZEST if you feel your guests aren't paying enough attention to you!

If there's a chance your garnish might brown, dip it into LEMON JUICE before adding it to your drink.

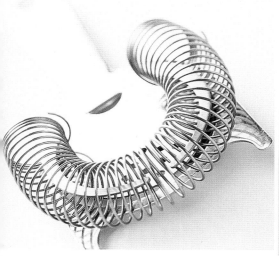

EQUIPMENT

For the aspiring home bartender, getting the right equipment can be as important as the taste of the final drink itself. You will probably find that you already have most of what you need to make cocktails in your own kitchen. But if you want to create the right atmosphere for your guests and mix cocktails with a little more flair, it's worth getting a few accessories.

MEASURE The measure is an essential piece of equipment for making cocktails. Measures come in a variety of sizes from the single shot of 25 ml to 175 ml for a small glass of wine. If you can find the inverted or dual measure (one end holds 25 ml, the other 50 ml) you are starting off on the right foot! Alternatively, your common or garden dessertspoon will measure a fairly precise 30 ml.

SHAKER The piece of kit most synonymous with the world of the 'spiritual advisor' is the cocktail shaker. While there are only two basic types of shaker – the three-piece (or deco) shaker and the modern-day professional bartender's (MPB) favourite, the Boston shaker – they can come in many shapes and sizes from the rather apt fire extinguishers to the abstract lighthouses and penguins! The three-piece (so named as it comes in three pieces; the can, the strainer and the lid) is the more suitable for home creations and for the more

ESSENTIAL EQUIPMENT

The modern dual-MEASURE/JIGGER measures both 25 ml and 50 ml quantities (a single and a double measure).

The Boston SHAKER, half stainless steel, half glass, is my preference for a stylish performance but the more orthodox shaker with the inbuilt strainer works equally well.

The BARSPOON is useful both for stirring drinks and for the gentle pouring required for layered drinks. The flat end can be used for muddling or crushing ingredients.

A MUDDLER is a wooden pestle for mixing or crushing sugar cubes or limes, for example.

A MIXING GLASS is used for making drinks that are stirred, not shaken.

Use STRAWS to test the balance of your drink, hygienically.

elegant world of the hotel bartender. Bartenders prefer the Boston shaker, purely for ergonomic reasons. Its two separate parts (the mixing glass and the can) allow the bartender more volume and yield greater results in the shake.

STRAINER Whenever possible, strain your concoction over fresh ice as the ice you have used in your shaker will already have started to dilute. If the Boston is your tool of choice, you will need something to strain the liquid out while keeping the ice in. There are two types of strainer – the Hawthorn strainer will sit happily over the metal part of the shaker while the Julep fits comfortably in the mixing glass.

BARSPOON AND MUDDLER The barspoon (or Bonzer) is the Swiss army penknife of the cocktail world. This tool comes in a number of styles; the long, spiralled stemmed, flat-bottomed spoon is the most versatile. As well as all the obvious uses for a spoon (measuring and stirring), the spiral stem and flat bottom allows its user to create layered drinks (see page 42). The flat bottom can also be used for gentle muddling (dissolving powders into liquid, for example). If more labour intensive muddling is required (extracting the juice from fresh fruit, for example) you may want a more user-friendly piece of kit. The muddler and the imaginatively titled 'wood' or 'stick' are more ergonomic and won't cause you as much discomfort as the Bonzer.

POURER Though not essential to the home bar, one of the tools that the MPB finds indispensable is the pourer (a thin stainless steel spout mounted on a tapered plastic bung). This piece of equipment allows us to pour a liquid at a regulated rate. MPBs count to a fixed number when pouring a spirit or liqueur to negate the use of a measure. Different liquors will pour at different speeds, however, depending on the amount of sugar in the liquid.

STRAWS For those of you starting off in the world of cocktails, a straw is an essential tool. In much the same way that a chef will always taste a sauce before serving it, you will need a method to hygienically test the balance of your drink. Dip a straw into the beverage in question and once submerged, place your finger over the top end to create a vacuum. Take the straw from the drink and suck the liquid from the straw – this small amount will be enough for you to determine whether your drink needs more sweetening or souring agent. This is called the pipette method and is used by bartenders all over the world when creating new drinks.

BLENDER Although the blender is an essential piece of kit for any bar, I'm not a fan of blended drinks. I'll make them, sure, but I'd rather make something that isn't instantly turned to watery mush at the flick of a switch. And besides, it's very difficult to entertain your guests over the noise of a blender at full speed. A prosaic kitchen blender should suffice. Try to use crushed rather than cubes of ice in the blender – it will add years to the life of its blades.

ICE Ice is another essential (and often overlooked) tool of every bartender. If you are making ice at home make sure you use mineral rather than tap water to avoid having chlorinated ice cubes. You can also experiment by adding certain flavourings to your ice cubes so that as they melt in the glass, the flavours are released into the drink. There are three different types of ice: cubed, crushed and shaved. Cubed ice will melt (and therefore add dilution) at a much slower rate but will also chill a cocktail less effectively than crushed or shaved. Drinks using crushed ice have risen in popularity recently, owing mostly to the arrival on the cocktail scene of concoctions like the Caipirinha and the Mojito. Shaved ice is mostly used in drinks that might require a little dilution to make them more palatable (remember, water is an important ingredient in a great many mixed drinks) and where they need to be absolutely as cold as possible.

OTHER USEFUL ACCESSORIES

A POURER (a thin stainless steel spout mounted on a tapered plastic bung) allows you to pour at a regulated rate.

A KNIFE is handy for preparing your garnishes.

A BLENDER will allow you to create iced drinks or to blend those containing raw egg or fresh fruit.

The JULEP STRAINER is a stainless steel strainer used when stirring a cocktail and pouring from the mixing glass. It is a versatile tool that can also be used as a less fine alternative to the sieve.

SWIZZLE STICKS for stirring drinks that have been 'built' into the glass.

A small TEA STRAINER can be used if a cocktail needs to be fine strained to extract unwanted ice chippings or the flesh or pips from fruit.

A great way to store your ice is in a PLUMBED STAINLESS-STEEL ICE CONTAINER, such as a sink, which keeps your ice from melting and sitting in its own dilution.

A LEMON SQUEEZER for extracting the juices of citrus fruit.

A BARTENDER'S FRIEND is handy for removing bottle tops and corks.

A JUICER is required for extracting fresh juices.

TONGS for handling ice.

GLASSWARE

Contrary to popular belief, you do not need to have an exhaustive range of glasses to create great cocktails. The glasses below should cover your needs.

The **SHOT GLASS** is fairly self-explanatory; it usually holds either a single or a double shot and is used to serve shots and shooters. It can also be used as a measure should you lose yours (a common occurrence even for the pros).

The **OLD-FASHIONED GLASS** (also known as the **ROCKS GLASS** or **TUMBLER**) is used for drinks that are served on the rocks (short drinks over ice). It should have a capacity of about 350 ml and can also house drinks like whisky and soda.

The **HIGHBALL GLASS** is a tall thin glass used for long cocktails and also for serving spirits with mixers. Anything over 350 ml should suffice.

HEATPROOF GLASS
Take your pick from the wine glass-shaped Irish coffee glass to the sort of tall glass in which you might get served a café latte in a smart restaurant.

You will need a WINE GLASS and a CHAMPAGNE FLUTE of some shape. As there is no real restriction on these you can be as ornate as you choose!

A MARTINI GLASS is a must for any aspiring mixologist. The longer the stem, the more ornate. Anything between 150 ml and 200 ml should suffice for drinks that are served straight up.

A MARGARITA COUPETTE is useful but not essential. This glass is also called the Marie Antoinette (so named as it is rumoured the glass was shaped around the curve of her breast).

The HURRICANE GLASS is a multi-purpose glass, which comes in a number of different shapes and sizes. Generally seen as a glass that holds punches and frozen drinks, it is also known as the TULIP.

TECHNIQUES

There are six basic techniques behind the creation of a cocktail – layering, building, stirring, muddling, shaking and blending. When creating a mixed drink it is important to remember two of the principles of cocktail making – first, to marry the flavours of the ingredients and secondly, to chill the ingredients. These simple principles can be applied to virtually any mixed drink. The only exception to this rule is the layered drink.

POUSSE CAFÉ OR LAYERING (1) Literally meaning 'push coffee', the Pousse Café was invented by the French (unsurprisingly!) and was served as an accompaniment to coffee, the two being sipped alternately. To layer a cocktail there are a couple of rules that need to be adhered to. First, and perhaps most obviously, choose liquors that will look dramatic when layered on top of one another in the glass. There isn't a great deal of point in layering liquids if they are of the same colour! Secondly, layer each liquid in order of density – this means adding the heaviest spirits first as they will sit at the bottom of the glass. The lower the alcohol content in a drink (abv) and the greater the sugar level, the denser the liquid will be. Therefore the sweetest and lowest abv liquid should be poured into the glass first. The higher the abv and the lower the sugar content, the lighter the spirit is. Be warned – this technique requires a steady hand. Pour your first ingredient into the shot glass. Pour your second down the spiral stem of a barspoon with the flat bottom resting on the surface of the liquid below.

BUILDING (2) Building is the process used to describe pouring a drink into a glass, one ingredient after another. It is the technique you would use to make a tall drink such as a gin and tonic or a Screwdriver. Once built in the glass, the mixture may require a quick stir with a barspoon or the addition of a swizzle stick. When building a drink always add as much ice to the glass as possible (see page 47).

1

2

STIRRING (3) When the ingredients in a drink are all alcoholic, the best method of mixing and chilling them is stirring. Stirred drinks should always be made in the mixing glass. If you have the time, chill the glass first by adding ice and stirring gently with a barspoon (make sure any dilution is discarded before the alcohol is added), or place the glass in the freezer for an hour prior to making the drink. When stirring a drink place your spoon in the glass and gently stir the ice in a continuous manner. Add all the ingredients and continue stirring until the liquid is as cold as it can be (about 0˚C). You may find it easier to strain the drink from the mixing glass using a Julep strainer.

MUDDLING (4) Muddling a drink may require the use of a barspoon, a muddler or a stick depending on the intensity of the muddling. As opposed to stirring, a muddled drink will invariably incorporate the

intentional dilution of ice at some stage. Whether releasing the flavour or aroma of a herb (such as mint in the Mojito), dissolving powder into a liquid (such as sugar into the Old-Fashioned), or extracting the juices of a fruit (such as fresh limes in a Caipirinha) the tool may change but the method is the same.

SHAKING (5) Drinks that contain heavy ingredients require a more aggressive method of mixing and chilling. You will find that a good, sharp shake will bring life to 'heavy' ingredients. Try building a Sea Breeze then shaking one if you don't understand what I mean! When shaking a cocktail there are a few things to remember. Whether you are using a three-piece or a Boston, make sure you have one hand at each end of the shaker and shake vertically, allowing the ice and liquid to travel the full distance of the shaker. When using a Boston the cocktail should always be made in the mixing glass, so those who are enjoying the spectacle of your labour can see what is going into the drink (it's not that complex guys honestly!). Add as much ice to the mixing glass as possible and attach the can squarely over the top to create a vacuum. Shake sharply until the outside of the stainless steel part of the shaker frosts over. When creating a shaken cocktail, always pour from the metal part of the shaker (it has a lip to stop the liquid dribbling down the outside of the vessel and the metal will help to sustain the temperature of the drink).

BLENDING You would usually be called upon to blend a drink when its ingredients involve heavy dairy products (as in the Piña Colada) or fresh fruit and frozen variations on classic drinks (strawberry daiquiris or frozen margaritas). Always use crushed ice in a blender and blend for about 20 seconds. When adding the crushed ice, the key phrase is 'less is more'. Add too much ice and the drink becomes solid in constitution (and what do you have to do? That's right, add more liquid!). Add a little at a time though and you can achieve the perfect thickness. Blending a cocktail will invariably produce an ultra cold, thirst-quenching cocktail. As the ice is crushed the drink will dilute or separate quite quickly though. Be warned, no one likes a slushy cocktail!

FLAMING Although not strictly a method of cocktail creation, this is a flamboyant means of adding a little theatre to the cocktail occasion. A liquid has to be over 40 per cent abv to light and even then it's often difficult to get the flame to catch. A simple way to overcome this problem is to warm the glass with hot water first. With overproof spirits (like absinthe), this will not be necessary. Be careful though, these spirits can often react quite aggressively and on no occasion should you ever try to ignite them from the bottle!

THE PERFECT SERVE

How many times have you been to your local pub or bar for a quick gin and tonic and instead of getting the quality of drink that you would expect from so simple an order you receive something far beneath the standard you would like?

This is what we in the business call the 'Queen Vic serve'. Although the standard of acting is high(ish!) on the soap opera *Eastenders,* the standard of bartending is not! One of TV's most famous pubs is guilty of making what looks to me to be the world's worst G&T and, at the same time, is setting a dreadful example to bars elsewhere. Surely no one in their right mind would ever drink anything out of those small wine goblets?! And not the slightest thought about ice? How about a garnish?! At least the tonic water is bottled but that's where the positives end!

Certain basic principles can be applied to make even the simplest of mixed drinks taste that much better. From storing your glassware correctly and choosing the right glass for your drink to knowing the amount of ice to add to the glass, the perfect serve is easier to achieve than you might think.

GLASSWARE When choosing the glass in which to serve your drink, firstly choose an appropriate size. For a long mixed drink, a 350 ml highball glass should suffice – or something large enough to contain the spirit and mixer as well as enough ice to keep the drink cold. For a short drink use a 350 ml old-fashioned or rocks glass. Ensure the glass is below room temperature with no smears or smudges and isn't chipped. It also helps when storing glasses to store them upright rather than face down as this can cause the air inside to stagnate. The glassware used for specific drinks is designed to suit the style of that drink. This is why the champagne glass is tall and thin (to maintain the bubbles longer), why the whisky tumbler is short and squat (to allow the drink's aroma to swirl around the glass), and why the brandy snifter is tulip-bottomed and slightly stemmed (to allow it to be warmed by the drinker's hand.)

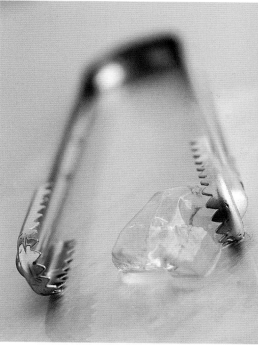

ICE If using home-made ice, remember to use mineral water. When ice melts it's water again – would you put tap water into your single malt? I thought not. If possible store your ice in a drained or plumbed area – ice that sits in its own dilution has already started melting and will not last as long as 'dry' ice. Always add as much ice as will fit into the glass (in the case of whisky drinkers, it's OK to bend the rules a little as they tend to be quite stuck in their ways!). You will come across two possible complaints with this ice situation. The first is what I call the 'McDonald's syndrome', where the ice takes up so much space that people feel they

are getting fiddled for value. The second concerns some of the governing rules of physics: the more ice that is in the glass, the colder the glass is, therefore the slower the ice melts. This contradicts the popular but erroneous belief that the more ice in a glass the more dilution there will be. A glass full of ice will read 10°C less than a glass with just the odd cube, allowing the drink to stay colder and stronger for longer.

ALCOHOL AND MIXER Try to use a premium spirit and a fresh mixer. The perfect ratio of alcohol to mixer is one part alcohol to four parts mixer.

GARNISH Always cut a fresh garnish for each drink. In the case of gin or vodka with tonic or soda, squeeze a wedge of lime into the drink, rub the fruit around the rim of the glass and drop the husk into the glass just before serving. When drinking an aged rum, with or without a mixer, try garnishing with a zest of orange for a more complementary garnish than the traditional lime. Don't overcrowd the drink with the garnish, cut a garnish down to size if it's too large (see page 35).

THE SERVE Serve a napkin beneath the glass to collect the condensation dripping down the outside of the glass.

THE PERFECT SERVE

Always choose a glass of a suitable SIZE AND SHAPE for the drink that you are serving.

Store your glasses FACE UP where possible to keep them smelling fresh.

Ensure the glass you are using is COOL AND CLEAN.

Try to work on a ratio of ONE PART ALCOHOL TO FOUR PARTS MIXER.

Think about the quality of the WATER you make your ice with.

Unless otherwise requested, add as much ICE as will fit the glass.

The more ice in the glass, the colder the glass and therefore the SLOWER the ice melts.

Always use a PREMIUM spirit.

Always cut FRESH fruit for a garnish. Use a new garnish for every drink.

Try SQUEEZING the fruit garnish into the drink or 'edging' the glass with the juice.

THE RECIPES

MARTINIS

Ferocious debate once raged over the best way to prepare the martini cocktail. Shaken or stirred, served up or down, with lemon zest or olive? Luckily, in these more tolerant times, the more creative mixologist out there has twisted and modified this iconic cocktail into numerous variations. Here are a handful of my favourites. Try the Breakfast Martini with your brunch if you need a revitalizing kick that won't taste out of place with a piece of toast, or a Pomegranate Martini if you like to kid yourself that a martini can be healthy!

ORIGINAL MARTINIS

CLASSIC martini

This is how I would make a 'standard' martini for anyone who requested one. Stirring the cocktail is a more authentic method and the original labour of love for any bartender.

a dash of vermouth (Noilly Prat or Martini Extra Dry)
75 ml well-chilled gin or vodka
olive or lemon twist, to garnish

Add both the ingredients to a mixing glass filled with ice and stir. Strain into a frosted martini glass and garnish with an olive or lemon twist.

SMOKY martini

This is a variation on the FDR Martini (see page 60), with the whisky substituting for the olive brine.

50 ml gin
a dash of dry vermouth
a dash of whisky
lemon zest, for the glass
olive, to garnish

Add all the ingredients to a shaker filled with ice. Shake sharply and strain into a frosted martini glass with a lemon-zested rim. Garnish with an olive.

CHURCHILL martini

Winston Churchill, like many of his contemporaries, would search for ways to prevent his beloved martini being sabotaged by the inclusion of too much vermouth. So, whereas some just aromatize their martini with vermouth and others marinade their olives in vermouth, Churchill would merely look at the bottle when fixing himself a martini!

(ALSO KNOWN AS THE NAKED MARTINI)
50 ml gin
1 bottle dry vermouth
green olive, to garnish

Using a mixing glass, chill a large shot of gin over ice and pour into a frosted martini glass. (An easier method is to keep a bottle of gin in the freezer.) Pass a bottle of vermouth over the drink, ensuring that the sun shines through the liquid onto the martini! Garnish with a green olive.

GIBSON

The leading theory behind the origin of this classic martini is that it was first made at the beginning of the 20th century for Charles Gibson, a famous illustrator, at the Player's Club in New York. Whatever its roots, this classic drink has truly withstood the test of time.

a dash of vermouth (Noilly Prat or Martini Extra Dry)
75 ml well-chilled gin or vodka
silverskin onion, to garnish

Add both the ingredients to a mixing glass filled with ice and stir. Strain into a frosted martini glass and garnish with a silverskin onion.

MONTGOMERY

This martini is named after Field Marshall Montgomery, a veteran of the Second World War. Considering 'Monty' fought in the North African Desert, it's surprising that he didn't prefer something less dry!

a dash of vermouth
50 ml gin or vodka
olive or lemon zest, to garnish

Stir both the ingredients in a mixing glass filled with ice and strain into a frosted old-fashioned or martini glass. Garnish with an olive or lemon zest.

VESPER

A shaken, medium-dry concoction, named by James Bond in the film *Casino Royale*. Bond christened the drink he devised after his Bond girl *de jour* Vesper Lynd.

60 ml gin
20 ml vodka
10 ml Kina Lillet (French vermouth)
long lemon zest, to garnish

Add all the ingredients to a shaker filled with ice, shake and strain into a frosted martini glass. Garnish with the lemon zest and serve.

HORSE'S

This recipe stems from the days when gin and vodka were considered medicinal. The ginger would have been added not only to flavour the elixir, but also to act as a herbal remedy to cure most ills.

12.5 ml ginger liqueur
50 ml vodka
lemon spiral, to garnish

Add both ingredients to a shaker filled with ice, shake sharply and strain into a frosted martini glass. Garnish with a lemon spiral.

MARTINEZ

The Martinez is believed to be the first documented martini, dating back as far as 1849 when it was mixed for a miner who had just struck gold in the town of Martinez, California. Its sweet flavours were geared to appeal to the taste buds of the time and the availability of certain spirits.

50 ml Old Tom gin
12.5 ml sweet vermouth
a dash of orange bitters
a dash of maraschino
lemon twist, to garnish

Add all the ingredients to a shaker filled with ice, shake and strain into a frosted martini glass. Garnish with a lemon twist.

ultimate martini

ULTIMATE martini

Every martini should be made using the very finest
ingredients. Make this martini the 'ultimate' by choosing
from the exceptional quality spirits now available.

a drop of Vya dry vermouth
50 ml well-chilled ultra premium gin or vodka
twist of lemon or olive, to garnish

Rinse a frosted martini glass with the vermouth and discard. Add the spirit
and garnish with a twist of lemon or an olive.

FDR martini

Franklin D Roosevelt carried a martini kit on international
summits. One of his specialities, which he mixed for Stalin
during a conference, was probably the first FDR Martini.

50 ml gin
a dash of dry vermouth
12.5 ml olive brine
lemon zest, for the glass
green olive, to garnish

Add the gin, dry vermouth and olive brine to a shaker filled with cracked
ice. Shake sharply and strain into a frosted martini glass with a lemon-
zested rim. Garnish with an olive.

the PERSONALTINI

As a lover of martinis of all shapes and sizes, it wasn't
easy to name my favourite but here it is: a naked black
Stoli martini, stirred and served up. Create and name
your own martini.

60 ml Stolichnaya vodka
2 black olives, to garnish

Add the Stoli vodka to a mixing glass filled with ice. Stir until the mixing glass
frosts and strain into a frosted martini glass. Garnish with two black olives.

FLAVOURED MARTINIS

cherry martini

RASPBERRY martini

This old favourite of mine should be quite thick in consistency, so if you aren't using purée, use a handful of raspberries to ensure it flows down your throat like treacle.

50 ml vodka
a dash of crème de framboise
a dash of orange bitters
12.5 ml raspberry purée
2 fresh raspberries, to garnish

Shake all the ingredients in a shaker filled with ice and strain into a frosted martini glass. Garnish with two fresh raspberries.

CHERRY martini

This martini can also be made using the juice from canned cherries – it may not sound as nice on paper but wait until you taste it! For a delicious variation, try using the juice from canned lychees – another winner!

3 stoned fresh cherries
50 ml vodka
50 ml thick cherry juice
a dash of cherry schnapps

Crush the cherries in a shaker using the flat end of a barspoon. Add ice and the remaining ingredients, shake sharply and strain through a sieve into a frosted martini glass.

STRAWBERRY martini

Use the ripest strawberries in this martini. The strawberry flavour is enhanced by a dash of crème de fraise (strawberry liqueur), but this should be kept to a minimum compared with the fresh fruit.

3 fresh strawberries
2 teaspoons sugar syrup
50 ml vodka
a dash of crème de fraise

Place the strawberries in a shaker and muddle with the flat end of a barspoon. Add the remaining ingredients, shake hard and strain through a sieve into a frosted martini glass.

POMEGRANATE

As this is one of the subtler of the fruit martinis, care must be taken to ensure the pomegranate is ripe. Try to avoid getting any of the fruit's bitter pith in the drink, as this would destroy its delicate balance.

1 pomegranate
50 ml vodka
a dash of sugar syrup

Spoon the pomegranate flesh into a shaker and crush, using a muddler or the flat end of a barspoon. Add ice to the shaker with the remaining ingredients. Shake sharply and strain through a sieve into a frosted martini glass.

CITRUS martini

Another old favourite, this martini needs to be shaken hard to take the edge off the lemon. Try substituting lime for lemon for a slightly more tart variation.

50 ml Cytryonowka vodka
25 ml lemon juice
25 ml Cointreau
a dash of sugar syrup
lemon zest, to garnish

Add all the ingredients to a shaker filled with ice, shake sharply and strain into a frosted martini glass. Garnish with the lemon zest.

FRENCH martini

This martini is great for parties as it is light and creamy, and simple to make in bulk. Shake this one hard when preparing it and you will be rewarded with a thick white froth on the surface of the drink.

50 ml vodka
a large dash of Chambord or crème de mure
75 ml fresh pineapple juice

Add all the ingredients to a shaker filled with ice, shake sharply and strain into a frosted martini glass.

PEAR martini

This fruit martini is certainly not for the faint-hearted. Unlike a lot of the fruit martinis, whose sweetness belies their strength, this one pulls no punches.

50 ml vodka
a dash of Poire William eau de vie
thin pear slice, to garnish

Shake both the ingredients in a shaker filled with ice and strain into a frosted martini glass. Garnish with a thin slice of pear and serve.

NEO MARTINIS

sake martini

polish martini

POLISH martini

The bitterness of Zubrowka with the potent sweetness
of Krupnik combine with the crispness of apple juice
to create a beguiling depth of taste.

25 ml Krupnik vodka
25 ml Zubrowka vodka
25 ml fresh apple juice

Pour the Krupnik vodka, Zubrowka vodka and apple juice into a mixing
glass filled with ice. Stir and strain into a frosted martini glass.

SAKE martini

This heady combination of gin, vodka and sake might not
sound very tempting, but take it from me, it's definitely
worth having a try next time you order that takeaway sushi!

25 ml sake
25 ml vodka
a dash of gin
olive, to garnish

Pour the sake, vodka and a dash of gin into a mixing glass filled with ice.
Stir the mixture until thoroughly chilled and strain into a frosted martini
glass. Garnish with an olive.

APPLEJACK martini

Inspired by recipes using American apple brandy, this drink relies heavily on the addition of Manzana Verde, a green apple liqueur that lends a bittersweet quality to the martini.

25 ml vodka
25 ml Manzana Verde
20 ml calvados
thin apple slice, to garnish

Add all the ingredients to a mixing glass filled with ice, stir until the glass appears frosted then strain into a frosted martini glass. Garnish with a thin slice of apple.

AZURE martini

Cachaça works amazingly well when mixed with lime and sugar in a Caipirinha, so it stands to reason that it can work well on its own.

½ apple
50 ml cachaça
12.5 ml canella liqueur
a dash of fresh lime or lemon juice
a dash of sugar syrup

Pound the apple in the bottom of a cocktail shaker to release the flavour. Add crushed ice and the remaining ingredients, shake and strain through a sieve into a frosted martini glass.

breakfast martini

BREAKFAST martini

This pretty much says it all for the versatility of vodka and the extremes to which bartenders will go to create something new and off the wall! It's probably best served at the end of a long night. If you fancy something a little more tangy, try replacing the orange marmalade with lime marmalade.

50 ml vodka
2 barspoons marmalade

Pour the vodka into a shaker filled with ice, add the marmalade, shake sharply and strain into a frosted martini glass.

BLOOD martini

A bittersweet concoction that needs to be delicately balanced. The lime juice and the Campari provide the bitterness, while the sweet element comes in the form of the raspberry liqueur. Taste the drink before and after adding the orange zest – what a difference!

50 ml vodka
15 ml Campari
10 ml crème de framboise
5 ml fresh lime juice
30 ml fresh orange juice
a dash of Cointreau
flaming orange zest, to garnish (see page 35)

Add all the ingredients to a shaker filled with ice, shake sharply and strain into a frosted martini glass. Garnish with a flaming orange zest.

LEGEND

Invented in London in the late 1980s, this recipe has to be followed closely as too much of any of the ingredients can result in an unpalatable cocktail. Make sure you taste each concoction before you serve it.

50 ml vodka
25 ml crème de mure
25 ml fresh lime juice
a dash of sugar syrup

Add all the ingredients to a shaker filled with ice, shake sharply and strain into an ice-filled frosted martini glass.

PONTBERRY martini

This martini is a snip to prepare as it involves no fresh fruit. Strong and sweet, it should appeal to a wide range of tastes.

50 ml vodka
75 ml cranberry juice
a large dash of crème de mure

Shake all the ingredients in a shaker filled with ice. Strain into a frosted martini glass and serve.

blood martini

pontberry martini

HINTS AND TIPS: the best way to chill a martini glass is to fill it with both ice and carbonated water

HAZELNUT martini

This martini has proved popular with men and women alike. A strong, clear chocolate martini with an undercurrent of hazelnut thanks to the Frangelico, it is perfect after dinner with a coffee – a dessert and a nightcap rolled into one.

50 ml vodka
20 ml white crème de cacao
10 ml Frangelico
grated nutmeg, for the glass

Add all the ingredients to a shaker filled with ice. Shake and strain into a frosted martini glass rimmed with grated nutmeg.

black BISON

The central ingredient to this mix is Zubrowka, a vodka that tastes of freshly cut hay, and lends a distinct quality to any cocktail. Combine this with Chambord and you have a truly memorable union!

4 blackcurrants
50 ml Zubrowka vodka
20 ml Chambord or crème de mure
12.5 ml fresh lime juice
a dash of sugar syrup
blueberry, to garnish

Muddle the blackcurrants in a shaker. Add the remaining ingredients to the shaker with ice, shake sharply and strain into a frosted martini glass. Garnish with a blueberry.

turkish chocolate martini

LIQUORICE martini

You need to infuse some vodka with liquorice as described below. For a stronger flavour, or if you're in a rush, pop the liquorice into a bowl of vodka and place in a microwave on full power for two minutes. It's not ideal as it does burn off some of the alcohol, but if you want to cut corners . . .

60 ml liquorice-infused vodka (see below)
a dash of Pernod
strip of liquorice, to garnish

LIQUORICE-INFUSED VODKA: Add a 10 cm strip of black liquorice to a bottle of vodka and leave for half an hour.

Pour the liquorice-infused vodka into a shaker filled with ice and shake sharply. Rinse a rocks glass with the dash of Pernod and discard. Fill the glass with ice. Strain the infused vodka into the glass and garnish with a strip of liquorice.

TURKISH CHOCOLATE

I've always wanted to find a credible drink that includes rose water, and here it is. The heaviness of the crème de cacao combines with the lightness of the flower water to create a truly Turkish delight!

50 ml vodka
10 ml white crème de cacao
2 dashes of rose water
cocoa powder, for the glass

Add all the ingredients to a shaker filled with ice, shake and strain into a frosted martini glass rimmed with cocoa powder.

TWISTED MARTINIS

SAPPHIRE martini

A couple of drops of Parfait Amour, a beautifully named
orange curaçao flavoured with violets, combined with well-
chilled Bombay Sapphire gin produces a magnificent cocktail.

a dash of Parfait Amour
50 ml chilled Bombay Sapphire gin
blueberries, to garnish

Gently pour the Parfait Amour into a frosted martini glass. Pour the gin
(which should have been in the freezer for at least 1 hour) over a barspoon,
so that it sits over the liqueur. Garnish with blueberries on a cocktail stick.

GOTHAM

A cocktail that is as sinister and mysterious as the name suggests. Try varying the amount of black Sambuca (one of the most underused cocktail ingredients I know) for a darker, more threatening result.

60 ml frozen Stolichnaya vodka
a dash of black Sambuca

Pour the vodka into a frosted martini glass, gently add the Sambuca, and serve.

BLACK dog

For those who love the idea of a martini but refuse to be budged from drinking rum-based cocktails (an honourable but distinctly narrow-minded point of view) the Black Dog is the answer.

50 ml light rum
a dash of dry vermouth
black olive, to garnish

Add the rum and vermouth to a mixing glass filled with ice and stir rhythmically and gently. Once the mixture is thoroughly chilled, strain into a frosted martini glass and garnish with a black olive.

THUNDERER

This cocktail smells almost perfumed. A hint of Parfait Amour and a tease of crème de cassis is all this drink needs to achieve its flowery, distinctive taste.

2 drops of Parfait Amour
2 drops of crème de cassis
60 ml frozen vodka
2 blueberries, to garnish

Pour the Parfait Amour and cassis into a frosted martini glass. Add the frozen vodka and garnish with two blueberries.

gotham

thunderer

JOE average

Despite its name, there is nothing average about this drink. Nor should the Pimm's in the recipe fool you – this is not a drink to be taken lightly!

60 ml Stolichnaya vodka
a dash of Pimm's No 1 cup
thin cucumber slice and lemon
zest, to garnish

Add both the ingredients to a mixing glass filled with ice, stir until the glass appears frosted then strain into a frosted martini glass. Garnish with a thin slice of cucumber and lemon zest.

RED star

The Red Star is a delicate drink. Ensure the glass is well frosted to highlight the hint of aniseed taken from the seed of this Chinese plant.

15 ml star anise-infused dry vermouth (see below)
50 ml vodka
star anise, to garnish

STAR ANISE-INFUSED DRY VERMOUTH: Infuse four star anises in a small bottle of Noilly Prat vermouth for two days.

Add the dry vermouth and the vodka to a mixing glass filled with ice and stir until the glass is frosted. Strain into a frosted martini glass and garnish with a star anise.

TEQUILINI

Chilled to perfection and softened by the vermouth, this cocktail is a great way to serve an aged tequila.

10 ml dry vermouth
50 ml premium añejo tequila
lime zest, to garnish

Add a dash of vermouth to a mixing glass filled with ice. Stir gently then discard any dilution. Add the tequila and stir again for fifteen seconds. Strain the mixture into a frosted martini glass and garnish with a lime zest.

CAJUN martini

A word of warning, this drink must be monitored while it is infusing. Habañero chillies are incredibly strong and should be treated with respect. A glass of milk will neutralize the effect if you overdo it!

60 ml habañero-infused vodka (see below)
½ pitted habañero chilli, to garnish (don't eat it!)

HANBAÑERO-INFUSED VODKA: Place three habañero chillies (with seeds) into a bottle of vodka and leave until they start to lose their colour – the more translucent the chillies become, the more flavour has been absorbed into the vodka.

Add the infused vodka to a mixing glass filled with ice and stir until the glass is frosted. Strain into a frosted martini glass and garnish with a habañero chilli.

COSMOPOLITANS

ginger cosmopolitan

CLASSIC cosmopolitan

The TV programme *Sex and the City* made this drink popular; its great taste has ensured it stays that way.

50 ml lemon vodka
20 ml triple sec
20 ml lime juice
25 ml cranberry juice

Add all the ingredients to a shaker filled with ice, shake sharply and strain into a frosted martini glass.

GINGER cosmopolitan

The mix of flaming orange zest, ginger, lime juice and lemon vodka gives this drink an incredible depth of taste.

50 ml lemon vodka
20 ml triple sec
20 ml fresh lime juice
25 ml cranberry juice
2 thin ginger slices
flaming orange zest, to garnish (see page 35)

Add all the ingredients to a shaker filled with ice, shake sharply and strain through a sieve into a frosted martini glass. Garnish with a flaming orange zest.

RUDE cosmopolitan

This drink earned its name following an evening that began well enough, but descended into heated debate. The tone of the evening changed when they started to drink tequila, hence the drink's name.

50 ml gold tequila
20 ml triple sec
25 ml cranberry juice
20 ml fresh lime juice
flaming orange zest, to garnish (see page 35)

Shake all ingredients well over ice and strain into a frosted martini glass. Garnish with flaming orange zest.

METROPOLITAN

This cocktail was one of the originals on the Met Bar menu. The blackcurrant vodka, combined with the cranberry and lime juices makes for quite a fruity concoction.

50 ml Absolut Kurrant vodka
25 ml triple sec
25 ml fresh lime juice
25 ml cranberry juice
orange zest, to garnish

Shake all the ingredients sharply over ice and strain into a frosted martini glass. Squeeze the oil from a strip of orange zest, held skin downwards and over a flame above the glass. Rub the rim with the burnt orange zest before dropping it into the glass.

BITTER cosmopolitan

The Cosmo should taste tangy, but using mandarin-flavoured vodka as a base adds a level of bitterness that brings even more flavour to the drink.

50 ml mandarin vodka
25 ml fresh lime juice
25 ml Cointreau
50 ml cranberry juice
2 dashes of orange bitters
2 dashes of peach bitters

Add all the ingredients to a shaker filled with ice, shake sharply and strain into a frosted martini glass.

STRAWBERRY cosmopolitan

Just to prove there's a cocktail out there for everyone . . .
If the Classic Cosmo is too sharp for your taste buds and the
Bitter Cosmo, just too bitter, here's the one for you. Make sure
that your strawberries are ripe and sweet for the best results.

3½ fresh strawberries, plus ½ to garnish
35 ml citrus vodka
25 ml Cointreau
15 ml fresh lime juice
a dash of cranberry juice, optional

Muddle the ripe strawberries in a mixing glass, add the remaining
ingredients and shake sharply. Strain into a frosted martini glass and
garnish with half a strawberry.

cosmo ROYALE

For a fizzy spin, add a float of champagne to this great
cocktail. The champagne will happily sit on the surface if
you have the patience to pour it gently!

35 ml lemon vodka
15 ml fresh lime juice
15 ml Cointreau
50 ml cranberry juice
champagne, to float
orange zest, to garnish

Add all the ingredients, except the champagne, to a shaker filled with ice.
Shake sharply and strain into a frosted martini glass. Float the champagne
on the surface and garnish with orange zest.

POWER APERITIFS

Traditionally, aperitifs were served before dinner to awaken your taste buds in preparation for the food on its way. Although we have lost the habit of taking a quick sherry at 6 pm every day, the practice of enjoying a citrus or bittered cocktail before dinner is still worth considering. It not only starts your evening in an appropriate manner but also allows you to forget the strains of work and enjoy your dinner.

PINK gin

Pink Gin is a thoroughly English cocktail which, although it originated as a medicinal potion in the British navy, became one of the smartest drinks in 1940s' London.

2 dashes of Angostura bitters
50 ml chilled gin

Rinse a frosted sherry or martini glass with Angostura bitters, add chilled gin and serve.

gin GIMLET

A great 'litmus' test for a bartender's capability – too much lime and the drink turns sickly, not enough and the drink is too strong. This one needs to be shaken hard to ensure a sharp freezing zestiness.

50 ml gin
25 ml lime cordial

Add the gin and cordial to a shaker filled with ice. Shake very sharply and strain into a frosted martini glass.

NEGRONI

The Negroni packs a powerful punch but still makes an elegant aperitif. For a drier variation, add a little more dry gin, but if a fruitier cocktail is more to your taste, wipe some orange zest around the top of the glass and add some to the drink.

25 ml Campari
25 ml sweet vermouth
25 ml gin
orange zest, to garnish

Build all the ingredients into a rocks glass filled with ice, garnish with orange zest and stir.

NEW ORLEANS sazarac

If, like me, you enjoy the lingering flavour of pastis, try adding Pernod to the drink rather than just rinsing just the glass with it.

25 ml Pernod
1 sugar cube
dashes of Angostura bitters
50 ml bourbon

Rinse an old-fashioned glass with Pernod then discard the Pernod. Put the sugar in the glass, saturate with Angostura bitters, then add ice cubes and the bourbon and serve.

ORIGINAL daiquiri

This classic cocktail was made famous at the El Floridita restaurant, Havana, early in the 20th century. Once you have found the perfect balance of light rum (traditionally Cuban), sharp citrus juice and sweet sugar syrup, stick to those measurements exactly.

50 ml golden rum
12.5 ml fresh lime juice
2 barspoons sugar syrup

Pour all the ingredients into an ice-filled shaker. Shake and strain into a frosted martini glass.

ORANGE daiquiri

The Orange Daiquiri substitutes the sweet Martinique rum called Creole Shrub for the Cuban rum of the Original Daiquiri so uses a little less sugar syrup to keep that delicate balance of sharp and sweet.

50 ml Creole Shrub rum
20 ml fresh lime juice
1 barspoon sugar syrup

Pour all the ingredients into an ice-filled shaker. Shake and strain into a frosted martini glass.

HEMINGWAY daiquiri

Legend has it that Hemingway was allergic to sugar so this drink was devised for him using maraschino liqueur as a sweetener (the sugar was returned to the drink when made for anyone other than the man himself!).

35 ml white rum
5 ml maraschino liqueur
10 ml grapefruit juice
15 ml sugar syrup
10 ml fresh lime juice

Add all the ingredients to a shaker filled with ice, shake sharply and strain into a frosted martini glass.

MULATO daiquiri

For those of you who like a more mellow daiquiri, experiment with aged rums until you find one that balances perfectly with the sugar, lime and your mood.

50 ml aged Cuban rum (such as Bacardi 8 Year Old rum)
20 ml fresh lime juice
2 barspoons sugar syrup
a dash of crème de cacao (optional)

Add all the ingredients to a shaker filled with ice, shake sharply and strain into a frosted martini glass.

SIDECAR

The Sidecar, like many of the classic cocktails created in the 1920s, is attributed to the inventive genius of Harry McElhone, who founded Harry's New York Bar in Paris. It is said to have been created in honour of an eccentric military man who would roll up outside the bar in the sidecar of his chauffeur-driven motorcycle.

50 ml brandy
20 ml fresh lemon juice
20 ml Cointreau
sugar, for the glass

Shake all the ingredients together over ice and strain into a frosted martini glass rimmed with sugar.

ABSINTHE cocktail

Absinthe is enjoying a revival in London bars after some notoriety in the early 20th century put it out of favour. The infusion of wormwood (absinthe in French) was believed to endanger health but any casualties were much more likely to have been the result of its high alcohol content. It can be as much as 70 per cent proof – so it's probably best to stick to just one!

50 ml absinthe
1 barspoon white sugar
50 ml still mineral water

Pour the absinthe into an old-fashioned glass. Dip the barspoon of sugar into the liquid, ensuring the absinthe saturates the sugar. Set light to the sugar and hold it over the glass until the sugar begins to caramelize, then drop the mixture into the liquid. If the liquid begins to burn, keep stirring the mixture until the sugar has all but dissolved (taking care not to crack the glass). Add the mineral water to taste, stir one last time and serve.

BACARDI cocktail

One of the best-known daiquiri variations and one that must be made with the Bacardi brand of white rum, as decreed by a New York court action in 1936.

50 ml Bacardi white rum
3 barspoons grenadine
juice of 1 small lime

Shake all the ingredients sharply over ice, then strain into a frosted martini glass and serve.

MANHATTANS

PERFECT manhattan

'Perfect' does not refer to how well the drink is put together, it describes the perfect balance between sweet and dry.

50 ml rye whiskey
12.5 ml sweet vermouth
12.5 ml dry vermouth
a dash of Angostura bitters
orange zest, to garnish

DRY manhattan

The least popular of the manhattans in my experience. The addition of dry vermouth doesn't lend the drink the warmth and reassurance that we expect from the manhattan's job description.

50 ml rye whiskey
25 ml dry vermouth
a dash of Angostura bitters
lemon zest, to garnish

SWEET manhattan

If you are unable to find rye whiskey for the manhattan, I would recommend experimenting with bourbon instead.

50 ml rye whiskey
25 ml sweet vermouth
a dash of orange bitters
maraschino cherry, to garnish

For each of the variations, add the ingredients to a mixing glass filled with ice (first ensure all the ingredients are very cold) and stir the mixture until chilled. Strain into a frosted martini glass, add the garnish and serve.

dry (l) sweet (c) perfect (r)

PREMIUM manhattan

In a perfect world every drink would be made out of the finest ingredients, but the cost means it's not always possible. Every so often though, it's worth splashing out and treating yourself.

50 ml Knob Creek bourbon
20 ml Vya dry vermouth
20 ml Vya sweet vermouth
a dash of Angostura bitters
orange zest, to garnish

Add all the ingredients to a mixing glass filled with ice and stir gently with a barspoon. Strain into a frosted martini glass and garnish with orange zest.

ANEJO manhattan

This is a Perfect Manhattan with tequila substituting for the whiskey. Try using all sweet or all dry vermouth instead of a combination.

50 ml añejo tequila
20 ml sweet vermouth
20 ml dry vermouth
a dash of Angostura bitters
orange zest, to garnish

Add all the ingredients to a mixing glass filled with ice. Using a barspoon, stir in a continuous motion until the mixture is thoroughly chilled. Strain into a frosted martini glass and garnish with the orange zest.

APPLE manhattan

The Apple Manhattan is a grand aperitif for the more discerning palate. This delicate cocktail may also be enjoyed after an excellent dinner.

50 ml calvados
15 ml sweet vermouth
15 ml dry vermouth
apple wedge, to garnish

Add all the ingredients to a mixing glass filled with ice and stir gently with a barspoon. Strain into a frosted martini glass and garnish with an apple wedge.

ROB roy

Bear in mind the vast range of whiskies available before choosing the one to star in this cocktail. If trial and error is your thing, you'll have some fun with this task!

50 ml Scotch whisky
20 ml sweet vermouth
20 ml dry vermouth
a dash of Angostura bitters
lemon zest, to garnish

Add all the ingredients to a mixing glass filled with ice and stir gently with a barspoon. Strain into a frosted martini glass and garnish with a thin piece of lemon zest.

MARGARITAS

The origins of this drink have been hotly disputed over the
years. Regardless of who actually came up with the margarita
recipe, the chances are that it evolved from the Sidecar – a
popular cocktail in 1920s Europe. It is thought that American
cocktail lovers would return from Paris during Prohibition
and head to the nearest place for a legal drink (Mexico). I
believe they took their knowledge of the Sidecar, substituted
the Cognac for tequila and switched the lemon juice for
lime juice. So began the life of the Classic Margarita.

CLASSIC margarita

Beware, there are young pretenders out there who do not treat this cocktail with the respect it deserves. Premixes, poor-quality tequila, too much ice and cordial instead of fresh lemon or lime juice all contribute to an unacceptable cocktail. Don't let your margaritas be tarred by the same brush!

50 ml gold tequila
25 ml triple sec or Cointreau
juice of ½ lime
salt, for the glass

Shake all the ingredients sharply with cracked ice then strain into a frosted margarita glass rimmed with salt.

TRIPLE GOLD margarita

Layered with a float of Goldschlager, the Triple Gold Margarita will bring a touch of splendour to any bar menu. Laced with real 24-carat gold pieces, Goldschlager is a cinnamon-flavoured liqueur that adds considerably to the depth of taste of the cocktail.

50 ml gold tequila
10 ml Cointreau
10 ml Grand Marnier
20 ml fresh lime juice
20 ml Goldschlager

Add all the ingredients except the Goldschlager to a shaker filled with ice. Shake sharply and strain into a frosted margarita glass. Float the Goldschlager onto the surface of the mixture and serve.

HORNY toad

Made using Sauza Hornitos tequila, the Horny Toad is named after the creature used to exemplify ugliness in Mexico. Are they saying drinking tequila makes you unattractive? (I've always found everyone much more attractive when I've been drinking tequila!)

35 ml Sauza Hornitos tequila
25 ml Cointreau
45 ml fresh lime or lemon juice
salt, for the glass

Add all the ingredients to a shaker filled with ice. Shake sharply and strain into an ice-filled margarita glass, rimmed with salt.

herba buena (c)

MEZCAL margarita

Choosing to substitute mezcal for tequila will impress any bartender. Mezcal tends to be more herbaceous and earthy on the palate – taste this drink and you'll find yourself whipped off to Mexico!

50 ml mezcal
10 ml brandy
2 dashes of Peychaud's or Angostura bitters
20 ml triple sec
20 ml fresh lime juice
salt, for the glass

Add all the ingredients to a shaker filled with ice. Shake sharply and strain into a frosted margarita glass, rimmed with salt.

green IGUANA

The combination of melon and tequila work perfectly here. I have chosen to use Midori (a melon-flavoured liqueur) in this recipe as fresh melon doesn't have the necessary sweetness to balance the drink.

30 ml Sauza Hornitos tequila
25 ml Midori
25 ml fresh lime juice
25 ml Cointreau
lime wedge, to garnish

Add all the ingredients to a shaker filled with ice. Shake sharply and strain into a rocks glass.

TEQUILA rickey

A long tequila cooler based on one of the oldest documented cocktails, the Collins. Add plenty of lime and sugar to ensure the drink has the balance and depth of taste it deserves.

50 ml gold tequila
25 ml fresh lime juice
15 ml sugar syrup
soda water, to top up
lime wedge, to garnish

Build all the ingredients in a highball glass filled with ice. Stir gently, garnish with a lime wedge and serve with two straws.

HERBA buena

This is a variation of the Cuban classic, the Mojito. Pack the glass with crushed ice and this cocktail makes the perfect summer drink. Add a little extra sugar for the sweeter tooth or a little more lime for a citrus twist.

50 ml gold tequila
15 ml fresh lime juice
1 brown rock sugar cube
5 mint sprigs, plus 1 to garnish
soda water, to top up

Muddle all the ingredients apart from the soda water in a highball glass using a barspoon. Add crushed ice, muddle again and top up with the soda. Stir gently, garnish with a mint sprig and serve with two straws.

green iguana

mezcal margarita

HINTS AND TIPS: put at least 10 lumps of ice into your shaker and shake the drink until the shaker is almost too cold to hold

TRES compadres

The combination of lime, orange and grapefruit juice provide the three citrus 'compadres'. Cointreau and Chambord are then added to the mix to sweeten, and lo and behold a great cocktail is born. Try serving this long (by adding more orange and grapefruit juice) for an extra refreshing cooler.

50 ml Sauza Conmemorativo tequila
20 ml Cointreau
20 ml Chambord
25 ml fresh lime juice
20 ml orange juice
20 ml grapefruit juice
lime wedge, to garnish
salt, for the glass

Add all the ingredients to a shaker filled with ice. Shake sharply and strain into a frosted margarita glass, rimmed with salt. Garnish with a lime wedge.

PRICKLY PEAR margarita

The prickly pear has become *de rigueur* in cocktails and makes a great addition to the margarita.

50 ml silver tequila
20 ml triple sec
20 ml lime juice
a dash of grenadine
25 ml prickly pear purée
thin pear slice, to garnish

Add all the ingredients to a shaker filled with ice. Shake sharply and strain into a frosted margarita glass. Garnish with a sliver of pear.

BERRY margarita

Anything from strawberries or cranberries, to blueberries or raspberries can be used in this recipe. Choose your own combination of seasonal berries for subtle variations.

50 ml gold tequila
20 ml triple sec
20 ml fresh lime juice
a dash of crème de mure
seasonal berries of your choice, plus extra to garnish

Add all the ingredients to a blender. Add two scoops of crushed ice and blend for 20 seconds. Pour into a margarita coupette and garnish with berries.

PINARITA

The combination of pineapple and tequila results in a truly tropical flavour. I will allow you to decorate it lavishly, despite my open disdain for garish garnishes!

50 ml gold tequila
20 ml triple sec
20 ml fresh lime juice
25 ml pineapple juice
thin fresh pineapple slice, to garnish

Add all the ingredients to a blender. Add two scoops of crushed ice and blend for 20 seconds. Pour into a hurricane glass, garnish with a pineapple slice and serve with two straws.

MANGORITA

This cocktail is an easy one to make, but very tricky to get right. Mango is a powerful-tasting fruit, which can overshadow the taste of tequila entirely, so take care not to add too much mango, especially if it is very ripe. Or do what I do and take care to add a little more tequila!

50 ml gold tequila
20 ml triple sec
20 ml fresh lime juice
25 ml mango purée

Add all the ingredients to a shaker filled with ice, shake sharply and strain into a frosted margarita glass.

RED cactus

The fresh raspberries and Chambord in this drink team up to provide a fruity punch that almost masks the flavour of its base spirit. Don't be deceived, there's still plenty of tequila in here!

50 ml Sauza Extra Gold tequila
20 ml triple sec
20 ml Chambord
35 ml fresh lime juice
4 fresh raspberries, plus 2 to garnish
lime wedge, to garnish

Add all the ingredients to a blender. Add two scoops of crushed ice and blend for 20 seconds. Pour into a margarita coupette or hurricane glass. Garnish with a lime wedge and serve with two raspberries.

raspberry TORTE

A successful cocktail needs to appeal at all levels. This one looks great on the eye, has a fresh lime and berry fragrance on the nose and, if you can ever bring yourself to consume your work of art, delights the taste buds.

50 ml gold tequila
20 ml Cointreau
20 ml fresh lime juice
50 ml raspberry purée

Blend the first three ingredients in a blender with two scoops of crushed ice for 20 seconds. Pour half the mixture into a margarita glass. Gently layer the raspberry purée over the surface of the drink to create a thin red line. Add the remaining blended margarita mix over the top and serve with two straws.

CHAMPAGNE COCKTAILS

In the early part of the last century, champagne was the most popular beverage in London for the discerning drinker. As a result, a great number of champagne cocktails hail back to those times. Champagne is the drink of choice for moments of intimacy, celebration and a sense of occasion and it is remarkably versatile in cocktails. It can be used with fruit to add inimitable sparkle, mixed with spirits like Cognac in the classic Champagne Cocktail, or complemented by the depth and flavour of liqueurs.

BELLINI

The Bellini originated in Harry's Bar in Venice in the early 1940s. Although there are many variations on this recipe, there is one golden rule for the perfect Bellini – always use fresh, ripe peaches to make the peach juice.

½ fresh peach, skinned
12.5 ml crème de pêche
a dash of peach bitters (optional)
champagne, to top up
peach ball, to garnish

Purée the peach in a blender and add to a champagne flute. Pour in the crème de pêche and the peach bitters, and gently top up with champagne, stirring carefully and continuously. Garnish with a peach ball in the bottom of the glass, then serve.

CHAMPAGNE cocktail

This cocktail has truly stood the test of time, being as popular now as when it was sipped by stars of the silver screen in the 1940s. It's a simple and delicious cocktail which epitomizes the elegance and sophistication of that era and still lends the same touch of urbanity (one hopes!) to those who drink it today.

1 white sugar cube
2 dashes of Angostura bitters
25 ml brandy
dry champagne, to top up

Place the sugar cube in a champagne flute and moisten with Angostura bitters. Add the brandy, stir then gently pour in the champagne and serve.

GINGER champagne

The ginger combines conspiratorially with the champagne to create a cocktail that is delicate yet different enough to appease even the most sophisticated cocktail drinker.

2 thin fresh ginger slices
25 ml vodka
champagne, to top up

Put the ginger in a shaker and press with a barspoon or muddler to release the flavour. Add ice and the vodka, shake and strain into a champagne flute. Top with champagne and serve.

ROSSINI

A great variation on the Bellini, the Rossini is spiced up with a little Chambord and a dash of orange bitters – two of a bartender's favourite cocktail ingredients.

15 ml raspberry purée
5 ml Chambord
2 dashes of orange bitters
champagne, to top up

Add the purée, Chambord and bitters to a champagne flute and top gently with champagne. Stir gently and serve.

MIMOSA

It is thought that Alfred Hitchcock invented this drink in an old San Francisco eatery called Jack's sometime in the 1940s for a group of friends suffering from hangovers.

½ glass champagne
fresh orange juice, to top up

Pour the orange juice over half a flute full of champagne and stir gently.

CHAMPAGNE julep

This cocktail works with all types of champagne or sparkling wine. If you have a bottle of bubbly that has been open for a while and lost a bit of its fizz, don't worry, the sugar in the recipe will revitalize it.

5 mint sprigs, plus 1 to garnish
15 ml sugar syrup
a dash of lime juice
champagne, to top up

Muddle the mint, sugar syrup and lime juice together in a highball glass. Add crushed ice and the champagne (gently) and stir. Garnish with a mint sprig and serve.

KIR royale

After a shaky start, the Kir Royale is now the epitome of chic sophistication (unless of course you prefer yours looking and tasting like alcoholic Ribena!). It started life as the Kir (a variation using acidic white wine instead of champagne) and was labelled *rince cochon* (pig rinse!). Luckily, the wine became less sharp and the drink adopted a more appropriate mantle!

a dash of crème de cassis
champagne, to top up

Add a small dash of crème de cassis to a champagne flute and gently top with champagne. Stir gently and serve.

black VELVET

I doubt if there is another drink in the world that looks more tempting and drinkable than a Black Velvet. Pour this drink gently into the glass to allow for the somewhat unpredictable nature of both the Guinness and the champagne.

½ glass Guinness
champagne, to top up

Half fill a champagne flute with Guinness, gently top with champagne and serve.

METROPOLIS

The Metropolis was a logical creation since the champagne and berry-flavoured liqueur combination was such an obvious success in the Kir Royale. Adding vodka gave a kick to that same seductive mix of champagne and fruit flavours.

25 ml vodka
25 ml crème de framboise
champagne, to top up

Shake the vodka and the crème de framboise together over ice and strain into a martini glass. Top with champagne and serve.

FRENCH 75

Named after the big artillery gun that terrorized the Germans during the First World War, rattling off rounds at a rate of 30 per minute. The popular variation on this drink was to mix Cognac with the champagne, which would make sense since they were fighting in France!

20 ml gin
10 ml fresh lemon juice
1 barspoon sugar syrup
champagne, to top up
lemon zest, to garnish

Shake the gin, lemon juice and sugar syrup over ice and strain into a champagne flute. Top with champagne and garnish with a long strip of lemon zest.

james BOND

The James Bond is a variation on the Champagne Cocktail, using vodka instead of the more traditional brandy. The naming of this cocktail is a mystery to me since the eponymous spy liked his drinks shaken not stirred, as in this cocktail.

1 white sugar cube
2 dashes of Angostura bitters
25 ml vodka
champagne, to top up

Place the sugar cube in a champagne flute and moisten with Angostura bitters. Add the vodka and top with champagne.

COLLINSES, RICKEYS AND FIZZES

A collins is a long, tall drink, designed not only to stimulate your senses but also to quench your thirst. It is believed to have been invented by a bartender named Collins who laboured at the old Astor House in New York. Made with lemon juice and sugar, the collins differs from the rickey only in the substitution of lemon for lime. A fizz tends to fit into both categories, using lemon, lime or any other juice variation and often including an egg white or yolk and a charge of carbonated water. Traditional recipes called for caster sugar, but use sugar syrup instead for more efficient cocktail making.

RASPBERRY rickey

This fresh fruit cooler always appeals due to the nature of the ingredients – there just seems to be something about raspberries in cocktails that everyone enjoys!

4 fresh raspberries, plus 1 to garnish
50 ml vodka
20 ml fresh lime juice
a dash of Chambord
soda water, to top up

Muddle the raspberries in the bottom of a highball glass. Fill with ice and add the remaining ingredients and stir gently. Garnish with a fresh raspberry and serve with two straws.

VODKA collins

Try the Vodka Collins for a sharp, zingy, thirst quencher on a hot day. Be warned, it's easy to forget there is alcohol in the drink!

50 ml Vox vodka
20 ml fresh lemon juice
15 ml sugar syrup
soda water, to top up
lemon slice, to garnish

Build the ingredients into a highball glass filled with ice. Stir gently and garnish with a lemon slice. Serve with two straws.

PEACH rickey

I sold a great many Peach Rickeys after devising this cocktail to use up a surplus of peaches ordered by an over-enthusiastic bartender. Ripe peaches will yield the best results if you're making your own purée.

50 ml vodka
20 ml fresh lime juice
15 ml white peach purée
a dash of crème de pêche
soda water, to top up
thin peach slices, to serve

Build all the ingredients into a highball glass filled with ice. Stir gently and garnish with a thin peach slice or two.

ELDERFLOWER collins

The botanicals in the gin get a bit of an unexpected boost from the elderflower, making this a delicate cocktail full of floral flavours.

50 ml gin
20 ml fresh lemon juice
15 ml elderflower cordial
soda water, to top up
lemon slice, to garnish

Build all the ingredients into a highball glass filled with ice. Stir gently and garnish with a lemon slice.

royal gin fizz

ROYAL GIN fizz

An offshoot of the original Gin Fizz, the Royal Gin Fizz has become fashionable in its own right. The substitution of the soda with champagne helps to make this cocktail special and lends it a little extra fizz – surely no harm there!

1 egg white
50 ml gin
25 ml fresh lemon juice
1 barspoon white sugar or 12.5 ml sugar syrup
champagne, to top up
lemon slice, to garnish

Put the egg white, gin, lemon juice and sugar in a shaker filled with ice and shake vigorously. Strain into a highball glass filled with ice. Top with champagne and garnish with a slice of lemon.

NEW ORLEANS fizz

The inclusion of rose flower in the New Orleans Fizz accentuates the juniper flavour in the gin, while the dash of cream gives this very light drink a little more body.

50 ml gin
25 ml fresh lemon juice
1 barspoon white sugar or 12.5 ml sugar syrup
12.5 ml rose water or orange flower water
12.5 ml single cream
a dash of egg white
soda water, to top up
lemon slice, to garnish

Add all the ingredients, except the soda water, to a shaker filled with ice. Shake vigorously and strain into a highball glass over ice. Gently add the soda water, stirring with a barspoon while doing so, and garnish with a lemon slice.

SLOE GIN fizz

You may need to play with the balance of
flavours in this cocktail. Different brands
of sloe gin have different concentrations
of sweetness and flavour – as is the case
with many liqueurs.

25 ml sloe gin
25 ml gin
20 ml fresh lemon juice
10 ml sugar syrup
soda water, to top up
lemon slice, to garnish

Add all the ingredients, except the soda, to a shaker filled
with ice. Shake sharply and strain into a highball glass filled
with ice. Top with soda water, garnish with a lemon slice
and serve with two straws.

SMASHES

I have categorized any drink that requires muddling (see page 44) as a smash. Remember that there are three different tools suitable for this job (barspoon, muddler or stick), depending on the level of effort required to extract the juice or aroma from the ingredient you are muddling. Don't try to muddle a Caipirinha with a barspoon, for example, as you'll find it much easier to use the larger sized muddler. Remember the work involved when you're in a busy bar at midnight – ask the bartenders for a smash only if you intend to tip them handsomely for their efforts!

CAIPIRINHA

Cachaça, a spirit indigenous to Brazil, is distilled directly from the juice of sugar cane. The Caipirinha has made cachaça popular in many countries.

1 lime
2 brown sugar cubes
50 ml cachaça
sugar syrup, to taste

Cut the lime into eighths, squeeze and place in an old-fashioned glass with the sugar cubes, then pound well with a pestle. Fill the glass with crushed ice and add the cachaça. Stir vigorously and add sugar syrup, to taste. Serve with two straws.

mojito

cowboy hoof

MOJITO

Guaranteed to whisk you away to warmer, more tropical climes, the Mojito emerged in London over the summer of 1998 as the thinking man's refreshing tipple.

5 mint sprigs
50 ml golden rum
a dash of fresh lime juice
2 dashes of sugar syrup
soda water, to top up

Put the mint in a highball glass, add the rum, lime juice and sugar syrup and pound with a barspoon until the aroma of the mint is released. Add crushed ice and stir vigorously until the mixture and the mint is spread evenly. Top with soda water and stir again. Serve with straws.

MINT julep

The Mint Julep originated in the American Deep South. Try substituting dark rum or brandy for the bourbon.

5 mint sprigs
2 sugar cubes
50 ml bourbon

Crush the mint and sugar cubes in the bottom of a highball glass. Fill the glass with crushed ice and add the bourbon. Stir the mixture vigorously with a barspoon and serve.

COWBOY hoof

The colour of this drink alone is worth the effort. Pay attention when straining the mixture as bits of mint sticking to the teeth are never attractive!

12 mint leaves, plus 1 to garnish
2 teaspoons sugar syrup
65 ml gin

Shake all the ingredients in a shaker filled with ice and strain through a sieve into a frosted martini glass. Garnish with a sprig of fresh mint.

black BIRD

The Black Bird is not a spur-of-the-moment type of drink. The work put in beforehand is in equal proportion to the look of amazement on its drinker's face. The Cointreau and the brandy in the mix draw all the juices out of the berries and they combine with the alcohol in a most un-alcoholic way. This is a drink to be wary of.

BERRY MIX:
> 1 punnet strawberries
> 1 punnet raspberries
> 1 punnet blueberries
> 1 punnet cranberries
> 25 ml brandy
> 25 ml Cointreau
> ½ kg caster sugar

50 ml lemon vodka
25 ml lemon juice
20 ml Cointreau

BERRY MIX: Add all the ingredients to a container, stir once and leave overnight. Stir once more before serving.

Place a scoop of berry mix into a frosted martini glass and press down. Pour the remaining ingredients into a shaker filled with ice, shake sharply then gently strain the mixture into the martini glass.

CLARET cobbler

A classic cocktail that can take whatever time throws at it. Choose red Bordeaux or Cabernet-Merlot blends for the claret.

lemon slice
lime wedge
orange wheel
30 ml claret or port
25 ml vodka
25 ml crème de framboise

Muddle the fruit in a shaker. Add the remaining ingredients, shake sharply and strain through a sieve into a rocks glass.

CHAMPAGNE cobbler

Champagne works with many complex flavours. If the fruit is not as ripe as it could be, add a dash more sugar syrup to encourage the flavour.

pineapple slice
orange wheel
lemon wheel
a dash of sugar syrup
champagne, to top up
mint sprig, to garnish

Muddle the fruit together in a rocks glass. Add crushed ice and the sugar syrup and gently top with champagne. Stir gently and garnish with a mint sprig.

PORT cobbler

Port has long been excluded from the world of contemporary cocktails simply because it is perceived as fuddy duddy. However, its full flavour works well in many cocktails.

orange wheel
lemon wheel
pineapple slice, plus 1 to garnish
75 ml ruby port
2 dashes of orange curaçao

Muddle the fruit in a mixing glass, add the other ingredients and stir well. Strain into a rocks glass filled with crushed ice. Garnish with a pineapple slice and serve.

CONMEMORATIVO

The Conmemorativo is a variation on the margarita using a premium, aged tequila. It was a New York band, the Fun Lovin' Criminals, who, during a night at the Met Bar in London, suggested that this special tequila could be used in a cocktail just as long as it was shown respect!

1 lime
12.5 ml sugar syrup
50 ml Sauza Conmemorativo tequila

Cut the lime into eighths, squeeze and place in an old-fashioned glass with sugar syrup, then pound well with a pestle. Fill the glass with ice and add the tequila. Stir and serve.

LAGERITA

A fave of mine, this is a drink for the more adventurous among us. It is essential that a dark beer is used. Apologies for the vulgarity of the name but the temptation was too great!

1 lime
25 ml Centenario Añejo tequila
1 brown rock sugar cube
Negra Modello, or other dark beer, to top up

Cut the lime into quarters, squeeze and drop them into a highball glass. Add the tequila and the sugar cube and muddle using a barspoon. Fill the glass with ice and add the dark beer. Muddle again ensuring as much of the sugar as possible has dissolved. Serve with two straws.

PASSION FRUIT batida

A lesser known cocktail that uses cachaça. This one is blended and, as a result of the greater dilution, not as potentially wobble inducing!

25 ml cachaça
25 ml passion fruit juice
25 ml fresh pineapple juice
a dash of passion fruit syrup
a dash of lime syrup
a dash of fresh lime juice

Mix all the ingredients in a blender, strain into a highball glass over crushed ice.

HIBISCUS martini

It's always worth experimenting with the Hibiscus Martini before serving it to guests, as the concentration of the juice can vary.

50 ml hibiscus cordial (see below)
25 ml vodka
a dash of lime juice
a dash of crème de framboise
an hibiscus flower or petal, to garnish

HIBISCUS CORDIAL: Dissolve 500 g sugar and 100 g hibiscus flowers (dried if out of season) in 2 litres of water over a low heat. Once the liquid turns a deep red, strain and leave to cool.

Add all the ingredients to a shaker filled with ice, shake sharply and strain into a frosted martini glass. Garnish with a hibiscus flower or petal.

FIXES

Fixes are similar to sours (pages 130–135) but have the addition of fresh fruit or fruit liqueurs to enhance the flavour, either as a garnish or a muddled ingredient. It is always worth experimenting with fruit in its fresh form. Have a go at creating a Fresca to see how bartenders have looked to the kitchen for inspiration with flavours. Even with the inclusion of fresh fruit, these drinks still need to be balanced with a souring agent – using grapefruit juice instead of citrus provides an interesting twist.

FRESCA

The Fresca was invented to be served long
with lemonade as a refreshing summer drink,
but for every drinker who wants their thirst
quenched there will always be two who want
their socks knocked off – and who am I to
argue? See opposite for a choice of
ingredients.

Add the ingredients to a shaker filled with ice, shake
sharply, then strain through a sieve into a frosted martini
glass. Garnish and serve.

BASIL and HONEY

50 ml vodka
a dash of lime juice
a dash of grapefruit juice
2 basil sprigs, crushed
1 teaspoon honey
basil leaf, to garnish

ORANGE and PEAR

50 ml vodka
a dash of lime juice
a dash of grapefruit juice
orange slice, crushed
pear slice, crushed
orange zest, to garnish

PORT and BLACKBERRY

50 ml vodka
12.5 ml port
a dash of lime juice
a dash of grapefruit juice
4 blackberries, plus 2 to garnish

DARK and STORMY

One of my favourite long cocktails
– warm and comforting with its dark
rum base but also zingy and
refreshing with the tried and tested
partnership of lime and ginger beer.

50 ml dark rum
spicy ginger beer, to top up
4 lime wedges

Build the rum and ginger beer into a rocks
glass filled with ice. Squeeze the limes and drop
the husks into the glass. Stir gently and serve.

gin BRAMBLE

This is a perfect cocktail for drinking
on a sunny deck in the cool of an
early evening.

50 ml gin
25 ml fresh lime juice
10 ml sugar syrup
25 ml crème de mure
lemon slice and blackberry, to garnish

Add the gin, lime juice and sugar syrup to a
shaker filled with ice. Shake the mixture and
strain into a sling glass. Fill with crushed ice and
pour in the crème de mure gently so that the
liquid sinks to the bottom of the cocktail. Garnish
with a slice of lemon and a fresh blackberry.

CUBA libre

One of the most famous of all rum-
based drinks, this was reputed to
have been invented by an army
officer in Cuba shortly after Coca
Cola was first produced in the 1890s.

50 ml white rum
½ lime
cola, to top up

Pour the rum into a highball glass filled with
ice. Cut the lime into four, squeeze and drop the
wedges into the glass. Top with cola and serve
with straws.

dark and stormy

cuba libre

LYNCHBURG lemonade

You may see variations of this recipe using triple sec or Cointreau as the sweetening agent, I prefer to use caster sugar for its coarseness and fresh lemon wedges muddled together for a more 'rustic' variation.

2 lemon wedges
2 barspoons caster sugar
50 ml Jack Daniels
lemonade, to top up

Muddle the lemon and sugar together in a highball glass. Add ice and the remaining ingredients. Stir gently and serve with two straws.

SOURS

The sour is a cocktail that works well with all spirits and many liqueurs, and I consider it my 'litmus' test for a new bar. If the bartender is canny enough to balance the flavours of the ingredients with sweetening and souring agents then the chances are pretty high that he will have an acceptable level of understanding for me to peruse the rest of the menu! Try making the Blueberry Amaretto Sour – it will always raise eyebrows and keep people coming back for more!

BOSTON sour

The classic sour is made with Scotch, but since I like my sours a little on the sweet side I prefer the vanillary sweetness of this bourbon-based version.

50 ml bourbon
25 ml fresh lemon juice
2 barspoons sugar syrup
2 dashes of Angostura bitters
a dash of egg white
lemon slice and maraschino cherry, to garnish

Add all the ingredients to a shaker filled with ice and shake sharply. Strain the contents into a rocks glass filled with ice, garnish with a lemon slice and a maraschino cherry.

sour ITALIAN

A cocktail made completely from Italian ingredients, the Sour Italian makes a good aperitif.

25 ml Campari
12.5 ml Strega
12.5 ml Galliano
25 ml fresh lemon juice
12.5 ml cranberry juice
12.5 ml sugar syrup
a dash of egg white
2 dashes of Angostura bitters

Shake all the ingredients over ice and strain into a wine glass.

KRUPNIK sour

The Krupnik Sour isn't really very sour at all because of the sweet vodka base, but altogether a most pleasant drinking experience.

50 ml Krupnik vodka
50 ml fresh lemon juice
25 ml sugar syrup
25 ml egg white
2 dashes of Angostura bitters
lemon slice and maraschino cherry, to garnish

Add all the ingredients to a shaker filled with ice. Shake the mixture and pour into a rocks glass. Garnish with a lemon slice and a maraschino cherry.

APRICOT royale

I would serve this one as shots to guests who I thought needed a bit of livening up! The fruity melody of flavours combines with the champagne to make this drink the perfect cure for the blues.

50 ml apricot brandy
20 ml fresh lemon juice
20 ml sugar syrup
a dash of peach bitters
a dash of orange bitters
champagne, to float
apricot slice, to garnish

Add all the ingredients, except the champagne, to a shaker filled with ice, shake sharply and strain into a rocks glass filled with ice. Gently layer a float of champagne over the surface of the drink. Garnish with an apricot slice and serve.

BLUEBERRY AMARETTO sour

If you want to add that special touch to your cocktail and don't mind putting in a bit of work, then infusing blueberry into your amaretto is well worth the effort.

50 ml blueberry-infused amaretto (see below)
25 ml lemon juice
15 ml sugar syrup
lemon slice and 2 blueberries, to garnish

BLUEBERRY-INFUSED AMARETTO: Pierce ten blueberries with a knife and place them in a bottle of amaretto. Leave them for a few days and taste. You may want to strain the mixture before using it.

Add all the ingredients to a shaker filled with ice, shake sharply and strain into a rocks glass filled with ice. Garnish with 2 blueberries and a lemon slice.

MIDORI sour

The words Midori and sour might not normally sit too
happily together, but shake this one hard, go gentle on
the sugar syrup and you'll have a great tasting, well-
balanced and dramatic-looking cocktail.

50 ml Midori
25 ml fresh lemon juice
15 ml sugar syrup
a dash of egg white
lemon wheel, to garnish

Add all the ingredients to a shaker filled with ice, shake sharply and strain
into a rocks glass filled with ice. Garnish with a lemon wheel and serve
with two short straws.

PISCO sour

Pisco, like cachaça, brings to light some of the delights
that are South American spirits. Tinker with the amounts
of lemon and sugar you put in this cocktail to achieve
your own perfect balance.

50 ml pisco
20 ml fresh lemon juice
15 ml sugar syrup
a dash of egg white
2 dashes of Angostura bitters
orange zest, to garnish

Add all the ingredients to a shaker filled with ice, shake sharply and strain
into a rocks glass filled with ice. Squeeze a piece of orange zest over the
surface and drop into the drink. Serve with two short straws.

HIGHBALLS, COOLERS AND PUNCHES

These drinks are grouped together because they are all refreshing options that contain either juice or carbonation and are served long. The slight oddball in this bunch is the punch. Punches are often the preferred drink for parties, made in a large bowl with any number of spirits, fruit and liqueurs added at random. Follow this formula: one part sour, two sweet, three strong (a spirit of some sort), and four weak (juices) to create a balanced punch while still affording yourself some creativity.

MOSCOW mule

The creation of the Moscow Mule woke us up to the godsend that is ginger beer. It lends the Mule its legendary kick and an easy spiciness.

50 ml vodka
½ lime
ginger beer, to top up

Pour the vodka into a highball glass filled with ice. Squeeze the lime, cut into four, into the glass. Top with ginger beer and stir with a barspoon. Serve with a straw.

STRAWBERRY mule

Perfect for an afternoon in the sun. Try substituting dark rum or bourbon for the vodka for a delicious alternative.

2 thin slices fresh ginger
3 fresh strawberries, plus 1 to garnish
50 ml vodka
12.5 ml crème de fraise de bois
a dash of sugar syrup
ginger beer, to top up

Muddle together the ginger and the strawberries in a mixing glass. Add the vodka, fraise de bois and sugar syrup and shake then strain through a sieve into a highball glass filled with ice. Top with ginger beer, stir and serve garnished with a strawberry.

BRAZILIAN mule

Try this variation of the Moscow Mule – great for an after-dinner drink.

25 ml vodka
12.5 ml peppermint schnapps
12.5 ml Stone's Ginger Wine
25 ml espresso coffee
a dash of sugar syrup
ginger beer, to top up
2 coffee beans, to garnish

Add the vodka, peppermint schnapps and ginger wine to an ice-filled shaker. Pour in the espresso coffee and sugar syrup to taste. Shake and strain into a highball glass filled with ice and top with ginger beer. Garnish with two coffee beans.

HORSE'S neck

Don't get too carried away trying to get the spiral of lemon either too long or too similar to a horse's neck – after all it's how the drink tastes that's important!

50 ml bourbon
ginger ale, to top up
lemon spiral, to garnish

Build the ingredients in a highball glass filled with ice. Drape the lemon spiral into the glass and over the edge. Serve with two straws.

PIMM'S cup

This cocktail is my one concession to the addition of elaborate fruit salad-type garnishes to a drink – anything goes with the Pimm's! Surprisingly, the tastiest addition to this drink is the cucumber, but try adding some sliced apple, too. I don't add limes to mine, though, as I find the strong citrus juice too overwhelming.

50 ml Pimm's No 1
250 ml lemonade
75 ml ginger beer
cucumber slice
lemon slice
orange slice
fresh strawberry
mint sprig

Build all the ingredients in a highball glass filled with ice. Stir gently and serve with two straws.

MADRAS

OK, you've stumped me, I have no idea why this drink is named the way it is. It's especially refreshing when created with fresh orange juice though, so perhaps it will become the mouth cooler of choice for those of us who enjoy a curry in or out!

50 ml vodka
cranberry juice, to top up
fresh orange juice, to top up
orange slice, to garnish

Pour the vodka into a highball glass filled with ice. Top with equal amounts of cranberry juice and orange juice and garnish with an orange slice. Serve with a straw.

TROPICAL breeze

A twist on the breeze format using flavoured vodka and fresh juices. There are a number of variations on this theme due to the ever-growing number of flavoured vodkas on the market these days.

50 ml Wyborowa Melon vodka
cranberry juice, to top up
fresh grapefruit juice, to top up

Pour the melon-flavoured vodka into a highball glass filled with ice. Top with equal amounts of cranberry and fresh grapefruit juice.

SEA breeze

The Sea Breeze is a modern, thirst-quenching variation on the classic Screwdriver. The cranberry juice lends a light, fruity, refreshing quality and combines with the bitter grapefruit juice, making it very popular with people who don't really enjoy the taste of alcohol.

50 ml vodka
150 ml cranberry juice
50 ml fresh grapefruit juice
lime wedge, to garnish

Pour the vodka into a highball glass filled with ice. Three-quarters fill the glass with cranberry juice and top with fresh grapefruit juice. Garnish with a lime wedge and serve with a straw.

MAI TAI

This cocktail has many variations. A thick, dark rum should be used along with all the fruit-based ingredients that lend it its legendary fruitiness.

50 ml demerara rum
15 ml orange curaçao
15 ml apricot brandy
20 ml fresh lemon
20 ml fresh lime juice
a dash of Angostura bitters
20 ml orgeat syrup
mint sprig, to garnish

Add all the ingredients to a shaker filled with ice, shake and strain into an ice-filled old-fashioned glass. Garnish with a mint sprig and serve with straws.

PLANTER'S punch

A Planter's Punch recipe can never be forgotten since Myers has very kindly put the recipe on the back label of its rum bottle. A great favourite for parties because it can be made in advance.

50 ml Myers rum
juice of ½ lemon
50 ml fresh orange juice
a dash of sugar syrup
soda water, to top up
orange slice, to garnish

Pour all the ingredients, except the soda water, into a shaker filled with ice. Shake and strain into an ice-filled highball glass. Top up with soda water and garnish with a slice of orange.

T-PUNCH

Perfect for a hot summer day, the T-Punch is a refreshing drink which can be made with more lime or more sugar, according to taste.

1 brown sugar cube
1 lime
50 ml white rum
soda water, to top up (optional)

Place the sugar cube in the bottom of an old-fashioned glass. Cut the lime into eighths, squeeze and drop into the glass. Pound with a pestle to break up the sugar. Add the rum and ice, then top up with soda water. Stir and serve.

JAMAICAN breeze

The Jamaican Breeze is testament to Jamaican rum's ability to hold its own when mixed with a selection of flavours.

2 fresh ginger slices
50 ml white rum
75 ml cranberry juice
75 ml fresh pineapple juice

Pound the fresh ginger and rum together in the bottom of a shaker with a barspoon or muddler, then add ice and the remaining ingredients. Shake and strain into a highball glass filled with ice.

RUM runner

The Rum Runner is a delicious example of rum's affinity with fresh juices as we've seen over the years in the classic Tiki cocktails and punches of Don the Beachcomber.

25 ml white rum
25 ml dark rum
juice of ½ lime
15 ml sugar syrup
150 ml fresh pineapple juice

Shake all the ingredients sharply over ice in a shaker then strain into a highball glass filled with crushed ice.

HINTS AND TIPS:
always use lots of
ice in a drink to
ensure it stays cold
and strong for as
long as possible

SALTY mexican dog

This is a tequila variation on the Salty Dog. It's a simple combination that can cut through the fog of any hangover with its trinity of grapefruit, salt and vodka. Try adding a dash of hibiscus cordial (see page 123) for a sweetened variation.

50 ml tequila
200 ml grapefruit juice
lime wedge, to garnish
salt, for the glass

Pour the tequila into a salt-rimmed highball glass filled with ice. Top with the grapefruit juice, garnish with a lime wedge and serve with two straws.

TEQUILA sunrise

A cocktail synonymous with the 1970s, bad hair, lava lamps and cheesy cocktails. Try modernizing the recipe by using Chambord instead of the grenadine for more depth. Alternatively, swallow your pride, slip into your flairs and enjoy.

50 ml gold tequila
200 ml fresh orange juice
20 ml grenadine
orange slice, to garnish

Build the tequila and the orange juice into a highball glass filled with ice. Gently pour the grenadine down the inside of the glass so the syrup fills the bottom. Garnish with an orange slice and serve with two straws.

HARVEY wallbanger

The story goes that Harvey, a Californian surfer who had performed particularly badly in an important contest, visited his local bar to drown his sorrows. He ordered his usual screwdriver – only to decide that it wasn't strong enough for what he had in mind. Scanning the bar for something to boost his drink, his eyes fell on the distinctively shaped Galliano bottle, a shot of which was then added to his drink as a float.

50 ml vodka
12.5 ml Galliano
fresh orange juice, to top up
orange slice, to garnish

Build the ingredients over ice into a highball glass, stir and serve with an orange slice.

AMERICANO

The Americano is a refreshing blend of bitter and sweet, topped with soda to make the perfect thirst quencher for a hot summer's afternoon.

25 ml Campari
25 ml sweet vermouth
soda water, to top up
orange slice, to garnish

Build the ingredients over ice into a highball glass, stir and serve with an orange slice.

SLAMMERS, SIPPERS AND SHOOTERS

These are the drinks that control the pace of a party.
During my days of running bars I would always keep an
eye on all of the parties in my bar. If I spotted a group
who weren't fulfilling their potential as guests of my
establishment (it should be a two-way street after all!),
I would entice them with a fun slammer (try the Tequila
Slammer and watch your party take off!), a gentle
shooter (easy to make in bulk and not too alcoholic)
or, for novelty value, a Pousse Café.

ALABAMA slammer

A cocktail immortalized in the film that every bartender loves to hate. What *Cocktail* did for bartending could only be countered by what *Titanic* did for ocean cruises.

20 ml sloe gin
25 ml Southern Comfort
20 ml vodka
100 ml fresh orange juice

Add all the ingredients to a shaker filled with ice. Shake sharply, strain into four shot glasses, and serve.

KAMIKAZE

A great drink to get the party started. Easy to make and even easier to drink, this is a low-maintenance shooter that does its job with minimum bother.

50 ml vodka
20 ml Rose's lime cordial
15 ml triple sec

Add all the ingredients to a shaker filled with ice. Shake very hard, strain into two shot glasses and serve.

pousse CAFE

Pousse Café literally means 'push coffee' and this was how it was originally served – as an accompaniment to coffee, to be sipped layer by layer alternately with the coffee.

grenadine
dark crème de cacao
maraschino liqueur
curaçao
green crème de menthe
Parfait Amour
Cognac

Layer a small measure of each of the ingredients, one on top of the other, in the order given in a pousse café or tall shot glass.

pousse CAFE 2

Another real labour of love. The Pousse Café 2 requires a steady hand and a steely resolve – especially if your guest pays little shrift to your hard work and chooses to down the drink 'in one'!

grenadine
anisette
Parfait Amour
yellow Chartreuse
green Chartreuse
curaçao
Cognac

Layer a small measure of each of the ingredients, one on top of the other, in the order given in a pousse café or tall shot glass.

TEQUILA slammer

The Tequila Slammer is the ultimate machismo drink and one that needs to be handled with care. This one is more likely to be imbibed for the sensation rather than the taste. A variation is to replace the gold tequila and champagne with silver tequila and lemonade.

50 ml gold tequila
50 ml chilled champagne

Pour both the tequila and the chilled champagne into an old-fashioned glass with a sturdy base. Hold a napkin over the glass to seal the liquid inside. Sharply slam the glass down on a stable surface and drink in one go as the drink is fizzing.

los tres AMIGOS

The salt, tequila and lime method is as ubiquitous as the margarita when it comes to tequila. Recite the immortal words: 'lick, sip, suck' – and enjoy!

lime wedge
50 ml gold tequila
a pinch of salt

Hold the lime wedge between the thumb and index finger. Pour the tequila into a shot glass and place the glass in the fleshy part of your hand between the same thumb and finger. Place a pinch of salt on the top of your hand next to the shot glass. In this order: lick the salt, shoot the tequila, and suck on the lime.

SUBMARINE

Forget those age-old constraints of spirit and chaser standing alone. Opt instead for the energy-saving Submarine and allow the tequila to seep gently from under its upturned shot glass and mingle with the beer before it hits the palate.

50 ml gold tequila
bottle Mexican beer (such as Sol)

Pour the tequila into a shot glass. Place the shot glass in an inverted beer glass so that it touches the base of the beer glass. Turn the beer glass the right way up so that the shot glass is upside down but the tequila is still inside. Gently fill the beer glass with the beer and serve.

DETOX

In the Detox, the combination of peach schnapps, cranberry juice and vodka is one that has been toyed with before, but layering the well-chilled ingredients allows the luxury of tasting them one at a time.

25 ml peach schnapps
25 ml cranberry juice
25 ml vodka

Pour the ice-cold peach schnapps into a frosted shot glass; over the back of a barspoon, carefully layer an equal measure of cranberry juice so that it sits on top of the schnapps. Over the top of the cranberry juice layer a similar amount of ice-cold vodka. Serve.

B52

The B52 has reached the lofty peak of being regarded a classic within the drinks world. This shot is best drunk after dinner as it has a tendency to take the palate by storm.

20 ml Kahlúa
15 ml Bailey's
15 ml Grand Marnier

Layer each ingredient on top of each other over a barspoon in a shot glass.

B50 who

The 'who' refers to the top layer of the shot. Explain the basic rules of the layered shot to your guests and let them choose their own *grande finale* to the drink.

20 ml Kahlúa
15 ml Bailey's
15 ml any spirit over 37.5%

Layer the first two ingredients in a shot glass, then allow your guest to choose a spirit to layer on the top.

BRAIN haemorrhage

OK, so this is one of the silly ones, but I had to include one! When made well this is a truly disgusting looking shot but your adventurous spirit will be rewarded if you dare . . .

25 ml Archer's Peach Schnapps
15 ml Bailey's
grenadine, to dribble

Layer the Bailey's on top of the Archer's in a shot glass. Dribble the grenadine through the Bailey's so that it settles on the bottom of the glass and serve.

SANGRITA

This drink is the perfect way to savour a fine tequila. Try varying the Sangrita mix, by adding different amounts of orange juice and spices.

50 ml añejo tequila
SANGRITA MIX:
   25 ml orange juice
   25 ml lime juice
   a dash of grenadine
   a dash of Tabasco sauce
   a dash of Worcestershire sauce

Pour the tequila into a shot glass. Add the remaining ingredients to a separate shot glass and stir gently. This drink should be tasted tequila first, followed by the Sangrita mix.

LEMON drop

There are various ways to present this shooter – you can coat a lemon slice in sugar and lay it over the surface of the glass to bite into after the shot or you can take it one step further and soak the lemon in Cointreau before coating it, then set it alight!

50 ml lemon vodka
20 ml Cointreau
20 ml fresh lemon juice
lemon slice, to garnish

Add all the ingredients to a shaker filled with ice. Shake very hard and strain into a shot glass.

PURPLE haze

The Purple Haze is a classic Kamikaze with a twist – a drink that belies its strength and will kick-start any evening's fun.

1 white sugar cube
½ lime
25 ml vodka
a dash of Grand Marnier
25 ml Chambord

Put a sugar cube and the fresh lime half, cut into quarters, into a shaker and crush them together with a muddler or barspoon. Add the vodka and Grand Marnier. Fill the shaker with ice, then shake and strain the mixture into a chilled shot glass. Float a single measure of Chambord onto the drink and serve.

sangrita

HINTS AND TIPS: keep your shot glasses in the freezer, the colder the drink the smoother the shot

purple haze

DIGESTIFS AND CREAMY COCKTAILS

I've always espoused the virtue of the cocktail being a means for anyone to find his or her drink of choice. The creamy cocktail may not subscribe to some of the laws of cocktail creation, but it is a popular choice for those of us with a sweeter tooth! A *digestif* or creamy cocktail can make a great alternative to dessert. Try the Vodka Espresso for a boost after a long dinner or the Orange Brûlée to experience the joy of a dessert in a glass.

VODKA espresso

With its dark velvety body and creamy top, the Vodka Espresso was designed both to wake up and to calm down its recipient simultaneously.

25 ml espresso coffee
50 ml vodka
a dash of sugar syrup
3 coffee beans, to garnish

Pour the espresso coffee into a shaker, add the vodka and sugar syrup to taste, shake the mixture sharply and strain into an old-fashioned glass filled with ice. Garnish with three coffee beans.

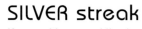

SILVER streak

Kummel is one of the least used liqueurs in cocktails, more's the pity. It has a distinctive, almost aniseed-like taste that comes from the caraway seeds used in its production and, as an added bonus, it promotes good digestion. For the best results keep both the vodka and the kummel in a fridge or freezer and pour them gently into a sturdy old-fashioned glass for the perfect after-dinner nightcap.

25 ml chilled vodka
25 ml kummel

Pour the chilled vodka into a rocks glass filled with ice. Add the kummel, stir gently and serve.

BLACK russian

The Black and White Russians are classics that have been on the scene for many years. They make stylish after-dinner cocktails with their sweet coffee flavour, which is sharpened up by the vodka.

50 ml vodka
25 ml Kahlúa
stemmed cherry, to garnish

Shake the vodka and Kahlúa together over ice and strain into a rocks glass filled with ice. Garnish with a stemmed cherry.

WHITE russian

The White Russian, with its addition of the cream float, is great served as a nightcap.

50 ml vodka
25 ml Kahlúa
25 ml single cream
stemmed cherry, to garnish

To make a White Russian, make a Black Russian (see left) then layer 25 ml single cream into the glass over the back of a barspoon. As before, garnish with a stemmed cherry.

BLUE blazer

A spectacular drink to serve but one that is best practised in the safe confines of the kitchen before trying it in front of an audience. Another tip for those of you who are itching to light up your favourite pewter tankards – unless they have heat-resistant handles, burnt fingers may be the result of your first attempt at this cocktail!

1 sugar cube
50 ml boiling water
50 ml whisky
grated nutmeg, to garnish

Warm two small metal tankards. In one, dissolve the sugar in the boiling water. Pour the whisky into the other. Set the whisky alight and, as it burns, pour the liquid into the first tumbler and back, from one to another, creating a continuous stream of fire. Once the flame has died down, pour the mixture into a warmed old-fashioned glass and garnish with a sprinkling of grated nutmeg.

RUSTY nail

This one's purely for the colder months, when you are curled up in front of an open fire, preferably with some sort of small four-legged creature curled up in your lap!

30 ml whisky
30 ml Drambuie
orange zest, to garnish

Add both ingredients to a glass filled with ice and muddle with a barspoon. Garnish with orange zest.

IRISH coffee

The trick to this great *digestif* is not to go crazy with the double cream. Sweetening the coffee does help the cream sit well, but if you don't take sugar it should still work – you'll just need a steadier hand.

35 ml Irish whiskey
double espresso
10 ml sugar syrup
250 ml double cream
3 coffee beans, to garnish

Mix the whiskey, coffee and sugar to taste in a heat-resistant glass, making sure the coffee is piping hot. Gently layer the cream over the surface of the coffee, using a flat-bottomed barspoon or a teaspoon. Garnish with three coffee beans.

MUDSLIDE

With the added kick of the vodka, you're looking at an after-dinner drink that will both caress your taste buds and lure you onto slippery slopes!

25 ml vodka
25 ml Bailey's
25 ml Kahlúa
20 ml double cream (optional)

Add all the ingredients to a shaker filled with ice, shake sharply and strain into a rocks glass filled with ice. Alternatively, add all the ingredients to a blender with a scoop of crushed ice, blend for 10 seconds then pour into a rocks glass. Serve with two straws.

HOT toddy

The Hot Toddy, with its warming blend of spices and sweet honey aroma, is the perfect comforter and will soothe any aches, snuffles and alcohol withdrawal symptoms that your illness may have inflicted upon you. It's also a great life-saver for cold afternoons spent outside watching sport. Next time you have need to pack a Thermos flask of coffee, think again – mix up a batch of Hot Toddies, and see how much more popular you are!

5 whole cloves
2 lemon slices
50 ml whisky
25 ml fresh lemon juice
2 barspoons honey or sugar syrup
75 ml hot water
1 cinnamon stick

Skewer the cloves into the lemon slices and add them to a heatproof glass along with the rest of the ingredients.

OLD-FASHIONED

Anyone who takes less than three minutes to make this drink isn't putting in the effort or the love required. This is the bartender's preferred cocktail to order on an evening out for two reasons. First, it's always rewarding to see a fellow bartender graft over one, and secondly, there is no better whiskey cocktail when made well.

1 white sugar cube
2 dashes of orange bitters
50 ml bourbon
orange zest, to garnish

Place the sugar cube in an old-fashioned glass and soak with the bitters. Muddle the mixture with a barspoon and add a dash of bourbon and a couple of ice cubes. Keep adding ice and bourbon and keep muddling until the full 50 ml bourbon has been added to the glass and the sugar has dissolved. Run orange zest around the rim of the glass then drop it into the drink and serve.

brandy ALEXANDER

The Brandy Alexander is the perfect after-dinner cocktail, luscious and seductive and great for chocolate lovers. It's important, though, to get the proportions right so that the brandy stands out as the major investor.

50 ml brandy
12.5 ml brown or white crème de cacao
12.5 ml double cream
grated nutmeg, to garnish

Shake all the ingredients over ice and strain into a frosted martini glass. Garnish with a sprinkling of grated nutmeg.

STINGER

A great palate cleanser and *digestif* which, like brandy, should be consumed after dinner. The amount of crème de menthe used depends on personal taste: too much and the result is akin to liquid toothpaste, another palate cleanser, but without the same effects unfortunately.

50 ml brandy
25 ml white crème de menthe

Shake the ingredients together over ice and strain into a frosted martini glass.

GODCHILD

Try serving this one long with milk for a less intense flavour. Grate some fresh nutmeg over the surface of the drink to add a whole new depth of taste.

25 ml vodka
25 ml Amaretto
25 ml double cream
grated fresh nutmeg, to garnish

Add all the ingredients to a shaker filled with ice, shake sharply and strain into a rocks glass filled with ice. Serve with two straws.

BLOOD and sand

This drink is quite simply the best-ever example of how a drink should never be judged by anything less than the sum of its parts. If this cocktail doesn't taste like your favourite festive pudding, you're doing something wrong!

25 ml Scotch whisky
25 ml sweet vermouth
25 ml cherry brandy
25 ml orange juice

Add all the ingredients to a shaker filled with ice, shake sharply then strain into a frosted martini glass.

orange BRÛLÉE

The Orange Brûlée is a dessert drink that should be savoured. You'll notice I don't recommend the caramelization process – would you trust a bartender with a blowtorch?

25 ml Grand Marnier
12.5 ml Amaretto
a dash of white crème de cacao
whipping cream, to top
orange zest, to garnish

Add all the ingredients, except the cream, to a shaker filled with ice, shake sharply then strain into a martini glass. Whip the cream and dollop gently over the surface of the drink. Criss-cross with thin strips of orange zest.

lemon MERINGUE

When set the challenge to create something special with Drambuie Cream, I thought I would bend the rules a little. Mixing citrus fruits with cream liqueurs generally isn't recommended for cocktails, but somehow this concoction resists the temptation to curdle.

50 ml Cytryonowka vodka
20 ml lemon juice
12.5 ml Drambuie Cream
a dash of sugar syrup

Add all the ingredients to a shaker filled with ice, shake sharply then strain into a frosted martini glass.

PINA colada

A sweet, creamy drink which, for a time, epitomized the kind of cocktail that 'real' cocktail drinkers disapproved of (compare a Piña Colada with a Dry Martini!). Today, cocktails are for everyone so there's no shame in ordering a Piña Colada at the bar.

50 ml golden rum
25 ml coconut cream
12.5 ml cream
25 ml fresh pineapple juice
pineapple slice, to garnish

Put all the ingredients in a blender, add a scoop of crushed ice and blend. Pour into a hurricane or highball glass and garnish with a thick slice of pineapple.

HONEY colada

Try the Honey Colada variation for a sweet surprise lurking at the bottom of the glass – only for the very sweet-toothed! Alternatively, use the Mexican liqueur Kahlúa as the base, for a light coffee taste.

For a Honey Colada, add 2 barspoons of honey or sugar syrup to a freshly made Piña Colada.

SILK stocking

This tequila drink was invented during the 1920s in the USA, at a time when cocktails were often given names revelling in innuendo and sensuality.

35 ml gold tequila
15 ml white crème de cacao
5 ml grenadine
15 ml double cream
2 fresh raspberries, to garnish

Add all the ingredients to a blender. Add two scoops of crushed ice and blend for 20 seconds. Pour the mixture into a hurricane glass, garnish with two raspberries and serve with two straws.

TEQUILA colada

This variation slips down the throat as easily as its name rolls off the tongue. Ensure this drink has the right consistency (light and fluffy) by adding crushed ice bit by bit to the blender.

50 ml gold tequila
20 ml coconut cream
10 ml double cream
150 ml pineapple juice
pineapple slice, to garnish

Add all the ingredients to a blender along with two scoops of crushed ice. Blend for 20 seconds. Pour into a hurricane glass and garnish with a pineapple slice.

GOLDEN cadillac

If the thought of this combination is too much for you, try replacing the crème de cacao with Cointreau to make another popular cocktail called the Golden Dream.

25 ml white crème de cacao
25 ml single cream
50 ml fresh orange juice
a dash of Galliano

Shake all the ingredients over ice, strain into a martini glass and serve.

GRASSHOPPER

An obvious combination of peppermint and cream, the Grasshopper is the perfect drink to accompany your after-dinner coffee.

25 ml white crème de menthe
12.5 ml green crème de menthe
25 ml single cream

Shake all the ingredients over ice, strain into a frosted martini glass and serve.

SILVER bronx

The Bronx dates back to the days
of Prohibition, when gang bosses
reigned and booze played an
important part in the economy
of the underworld. Different areas
of New York became known for the
special cocktails they offered, such
as this speciality of the Bronx.

50 ml gin
a dash of dry vermouth
a dash of sweet vermouth
50 ml fresh orange juice
1 egg white

Shake all the ingredients vigorously over ice
and strain into a chilled cocktail glass.

GOLDEN bronx

Like the Manhattan, the Bronx has
three variations: the dry, the sweet
and the perfect. The Silver and
Golden Bronx are variations on the
perfect with the addition of egg
white or egg yolk.

50 ml gin
a dash of dry vermouth
a dash of sweet vermouth
50 ml fresh orange juice
1 egg yolk

Shake all the ingredients vigorously over ice
and strain into a chilled cocktail glass.

MORNING AFTER

What the bartender giveth, he also taketh away. If you wake up in the morning feeling like you've been in the wars, you could either ignore the situation and simply go back to bed or you could take responsibility for your actions and do something about it. Most of my hangover cures are 'make or break' – they'll either put you back to bed or sort you right out! On a more serious note, the best way to avoid a hangover is to drink a glass of water for every alcoholic drink you enjoy through the night.

GAZPACHO

This savoury drink might sound like a strange
choice, but trust me it works! The Gazpacho
came about when a friend and I were out
for brunch and were looking for a change
of drink from the Bloody Mary. Gazpacho
was on the menu, so we put two and two
together *et voila*!

50 ml pepper vodka
black pepper, to taste
200 ml gazpacho soup
chopped herbs, to garnish

Shake all the ingredients really hard with ice and strain into
a martini glass. Sprinkle over some chopped herbs to garnish.

RED snapper

Red Snapper was the name given to the
Bloody Mary in the 1940s when the original
was deemed too risqué. I've taken the name
but changed the format.

50 ml gin
75 ml tomato juice
4 dashes of Tabasco
a pinch of celery salt
2 dashes of lemon juice
a pinch of ground black pepper
4 dashes of Worcestershire sauce
black pepper or lemon zest, to garnish

Add all the ingredients to a shaker filled with ice, shake
sharply then strain into a frosted martini glass. Garnish
with a sprinkling of black pepper or lemon zest.

bloody MARY

Curing hangovers can be painless, and should be enjoyable, too. The objective of a hangover cure is to get you back on that 'horse' straight away before you spend too much time reflecting on your early morning pledge never drink again! The measurements below depend on personal likes and dislikes.

50 ml vodka
200 ml tomato juice
2 grinds of black pepper
2 dashes of Worcestershire sauce
2 dashes of Tabasco sauce
2 dashes of fresh lemon juice
1 barspoon horseradish sauce
1 celery stick, to garnish

Shake all the ingredients over ice and strain into a highball glass filled with ice. Garnish with a celery stick.

LIVER recovery

Between them, apples, strawberries and bananas contain more nutrients and healing properties than I could fit on this page. What's even better, this drink tastes great!

2 green apples
6 fresh strawberries
1 banana

Peel, core, top and tail the assembled fruits, as necessary. Put each of them through a juicer, collecting the resulting juice. Add the juices to a blender filled with one scoop of crushed ice. Blend and pour into a small highball glass.

PRAIRIE oyster

This is one of those drinks that you have to try at least once in your life. It is best drunk quickly 'in one' – for obvious reasons.

a dash of olive oil
egg yolk
a dash of Tabasco sauce
2 dashes of Worcestershire sauce
2 dashes of vinegar or lemon juice
salt and pepper

Rinse a martini glass with the olive oil and carefully add the egg yolk. Add the seasoning to taste and serve.

CORPSE reviver

The Corpse Reviver will either ease your suffering completely or send you back to sleep!

25 ml calvados
25 ml vermouth rosso
25 ml brandy
orange slice, to serve

Shake the ingredients over ice and strain into a frosted martini glass. Garnish with a slice of orange and serve.

vodka stinger (l) stormy weather (r)

prairie oyster (l) corpse reviver (r)

STORMY weather

The Stormy Weather is well qualified to treat your hangover with its good measure of Fernet Branca, a very bitter *digestif* that is often used on its own as a hangover cure.

25 ml Fernet Branca
25 ml dry vermouth
2 dashes of crème de menthe
mint sprig, to garnish

Shake all the ingredients over ice, strain into a small highball glass filled with ice and garnish with a sprig of mint.

VODKA stinger

This gives your mouth a minty freshness that will at least banish any lingering night-before tastes.

50 ml vodka
a large dash of white crème de menthe

Shake the ingredients over ice and strain into a martini glass.

MOCKTAILS

Just because someone chooses not to drink alcohol (whether willingly or in their role as designated driver) they shouldn't be relegated to drinking water. With increasing emphasis on responsible drinking and the growing range of delightful non-alcoholic cocktails on most bar menus, there's no shortage of choice when not drinking alcohol. If I'm organizing a cocktail menu for weddings or parties where a range of ages are expected I always add half as many mocktails as cocktails to keep the more restrained among us happy!

CRANBERRY cooler

It's so simple, I defy anyone not to admit that this drink, when served ice cold and in the right proportions, is the only thing that almost beats a Ribena made just right!

soda water
cranberry juice
1 lime

Fill a tall highball glass with crushed ice. Pour in equal parts of soda water and then cranberry juice. Garnish with a squeeze of lime and serve with two straws.

ST CLEMENT'S

The name is taken from the English nursery rhyme 'Oranges and Lemons said the bells of St Clement's'.

bitter lemon
fresh orange juice
lemon slice, to garnish

Build both ingredients (the bitter lemon first) in equal parts into a highball glass filled with ice. Stir gently, garnish with a lemon slice and serve with two straws.

RED BERRY smoothie

I would like to thank Elsa Petersen-Schepelern for this marvellous drink. Even people with dairy intolerance are often able to eat and drink yoghurt, since it changes its structure during fermentation.

1 punnet berries (about 250 g),
    such as strawberries, cranberries,
    red currants or raspberries (for a pink smoothie) or
    blackberries and blueberries (for a blue smoothie)
250 ml plain yoghurt
125 ml crushed ice
Serves 2–3

Put all the ingredients in a blender and work to a thin, frothy cream. If too thick, add water to create a pourable consistency.

VIRGIN banana colada

This one works both as a meal and a drink!
To make it alcoholic, add a large measure
of Bailey's, which adds a kick and makes
the drink even more viscous.

1 ripe banana, reserving 1 slice to garnish
20 ml coconut cream
10 ml double cream
150 ml pineapple juice

Add all the ingredients to a blender with a scoop
of crushed ice and blend for 20 seconds. Pour into
a hurricane glass and garnish with a banana slice.
Serve with two straws.

VIRGIN mojito

There's nothing in the manual that says cocktails with no alcohol in them should be low maintenance or one-dimensional. This one is a way of saying thank you to anyone who has taken on the noble role of designated driver for the night.

6 mint sprigs, plus 1 to garnish
1 barspoon caster sugar
2 lime wedges
soda water, to top up
a dash of sugar syrup

Muddle the mint, sugar and lime in a highball glass filled with ice. Fill with crushed ice, top with soda water and muddle gently. Add sugar syrup to taste, garnish with a mint sprig and serve with two straws.

ICED tea

There is nothing more satisfying to make than a good Iced Tea. I know, as I had a protracted debate about the best way with a colleague – it wasn't until he conceded that mine was better than his that I really savoured both the moment and the drink!

4 tea bags
2.4 litres hot water
1 lemon
sugar, to taste

Add the tea bags to a jug of hot, but not boiling, water. Stir, take out the tea bags and leave the tea to cool and stand before adding fresh lemon slices and chilling in the fridge. Once chilled, pour the tea into four highball glasses filled with ice. Add sugar to taste and serve with two straws.

VIRGIN mary

Since this variation of the Bloody Mary is without vodka, I tend to go a bit crazy on the spices to compensate!

300 ml tomato juice
2 grinds of black pepper
2 dashes of Tabasco sauce
2 dashes of Worcestershire sauce
2 dashes of fresh lemon juice
1 barspoon horseradish sauce
celery stick, to garnish

Shake all the ingredients over ice and strain into a highball glass filled with ice. Garnish with a celery stick.

SHIRLEY temple

A thirst quencher for the very sweet-toothed and, most appropriately, named after the famous Hollywood child actress.

25 ml grenadine
ginger ale or lemonade, to top up
lemon slice, to garnish

Pour the grenadine into a highball glass filled with ice and top with either ginger ale or lemonade. Garnish with a slice of lemon and serve.

PUSSY foot

Try using freshly squeezed pineapple juice instead of grapefruit for a slightly sweeter variation.

150 ml fresh orange juice
150 ml fresh grapefruit juice
a dash of grenadine
2 dashes of fresh lemon juice

Shake the ingredients well over ice and strain into a highball glass filled with ice.

OLD-FASHIONED lemonade

There's nothing quite like old school lemonade. On a hot day, try using soda water instead of water for that extra zing.

25 ml fresh lemon juice
50 ml sugar syrup
150 ml water
lemon wedge, to garnish

Add all the ingredients to a shaker filled with ice, shake sharply then strain into a highball glass filled with ice. Garnish with a lemon wedge and serve.

GLOSSARY

ABSINTHE A very strong, green or yellow spirit made from wormwood (*Artemisia absinthium* in Latin, which gives absinthe its name) and flavoured with other botanicals including anise.

ABV Alcohol by volume. The percentage of alcohol by volume (ABV) indicates the strength of an alcoholic beverage and is shown on the bottle's label. Wine, for example, is about 11% ABV.

AMARETTO An amber-coloured liqueur of Italian origin, made from apricots and almonds.

ANISETTE An anise-flavoured liqueur of French origin.

ARCHER'S PEACH SCHNAPPS A colourless, very sweet, peach-flavoured liqueur.

BACARDI A well-known brand of rum, which originated in Cuba in the 19th century. The company now produces a range of different rums but the Bacardi name is synonymous with its original white rum.

BAILEY'S IRISH CREAM An Irish whiskey and cream liqueur with a lower alcohol content than most liqueurs.

BITTERS A potent herbal or fruit-flavoured alcoholic essence added to drinks in tiny amounts for its distinctive flavour. The original and most widely used bitters, Angostura, was first produced in the 1820s and is now produced in Trinidad. It has a rum base and is flavoured with herbs but details of the recipe are a closely guarded secret. Peychaud's bitters is an American brand invented in the 18th century by Antoine Peychaud. Orange bitters is flavoured with orange peel and other botanicals; peach bitters is another type available.

BLENDING A cocktail-making technique, which involves combining ingredients using an electric blender.

BOTANICALS Fruits, herb and spices (for example juniper berries, citrus peel, cardamom, angelica and coriander seeds) widely used as flavourings in the manufacture of various spirits.

BOURBON See 'Whisky'.

BRANDY An alcoholic spirit distilled from grape wine (ordinary brandy) or fermented mash of fruit (fruit brandy like apricot and cherry brandy). Fruit brandy is also known as eau de vie and tends to be unaged. True brandy is produced in every wine-growing region of the world, but the best comes from France, for example Cognac and Armagnac. V.S. ('very special') or three stars on the label indicates the brandy has been aged for a minimum of 2 ½ years; V.S.O.P ('very special old and pale') or Reserve denotes brandy that has been aged for a minimum of 4 ½ years; Napoleon or X.O. ('extra old') denotes brandy that has been aged for at least 6 ½ years old.

BUILDING A cocktail-making technique, which involves pouring the liquid ingredients into a glass, one at a time.

CACHAÇA A Brazilian spirit distilled directly from the juice of sugar cane (unlike rum, which is distilled from the molasses).

CALVADOS An aged French apple brandy from Normandy.

CAMPARI A vivid red, bitter-tasting Italian aperitif made from the peel of Seville oranges, herbs and quinine and first created in the 19th century.

CANNELLA LIQUEUR A cinnamon-flavoured Italian liqueur.

CHAMBORD A French liqueur made from small black raspberries.

CHAMPAGNE A sparkling wine from the Champagne region of France. Sparkling wines produced elsewhere by the same method are labelled 'Méthode Champenoise' and include Cava (which is Spanish), Spumante (Italian) and Sekt (German).

CHARTREUSE A potent herb-based liqueur created by French Carthusian monks according to an ancient secret recipe. There are two versions – the green is stronger than the yellow.

COCONUT CREAM/MILK Ingredients derived from fresh coconut, used in cooking as well as for cocktails.

COGNAC A high-quality French brandy from the Cognac region in the south-west of France, first produced in the 19th century.

COINTREAU A colourless French liqueur made from oranges and similar to curaçao.

CORDIAL A fruit concentrate, or syrup, usually diluted with water before being drunk. Elderflower cordial is made from the flowers of the elderflower tree; Rose's, the best-known brand of lime cordial, is made from West Indian limes. See also 'Liqueur'.

CRÈME DE BANANES A brandy-based liqueur made from bananas.

CRÈME DE CACAO A chocolate-flavoured liqueur, available in white (colourless) and brown versions.

CRÈME DE CASSIS A sweet liqueur of French origin made from blackcurrants, often simply referred to as 'cassis'.

CRÈME DE FRAISE A liqueur of French origin made from strawberries. Crème de fraise de bois is made from wild strawberries.

CRÈME DE FRAMBOISE A liqueur of French origin made from raspberries.

CRÈME DE MENTHE A very sweet peppermint liqueur of French origin, which comes in green and white (colourless) versions.

CRÈME DE MURE A liqueur made from wild blackberries, often interchangeable with Chambord.

CRÈME DE PÊCHE A liqueur made from peaches.

CREOLE SHRUB A sweet orange-flavoured rum from the West Indies.

CURAÇAO An orange-flavoured liqueur of Caribbean origin, made from Seville oranges and available in colourless, blue, orange and green versions.

DRAMBUIE A Scotch whisky liqueur flavoured with heather and honey. Drambuie Cream is the cream version of the liqueur.

EAU DE VIE See 'Brandy'.

FRANGELICO An Italian hazelnut liqueur, apparently created by an Italian monk, Fra Angelico, who lived in Piedmont in northern Italy in the 17th century.

FROSTING A cocktail-garnishing technique, which involves decorating the rim of a glass with salt, sugar, cocoa powder or grated nutmeg.

FRUIT JUICE A soft drink made from fruit concentrate, water and sugar, or juice that has been freshly extracted from fruit. Stick to the type of juice the recipe calls for – a carton of juice is no substitute for freshly squeezed fruit juice nor vice versa.

GALLIANO A pale yellow, herb-based Italian liqueur.

GIN A colourless grain spirit flavoured with botanicals, the main one being juniper berries. Distilled gin is the best-quality gin; be aware that some cheap

brands have been 'cold infused' rather than distilled. London dry gin is the most popular type of gin today, although sweeter gins like Old Tom gin were more popular in the past.

GINGER ALE A sweet, non-alcoholic ginger-flavoured fizzy drink.

GINGER BEER A slightly alcoholic drink made from fermented root ginger.

GINGER LIQUEUR A ginger-flavoured liqueur. Dutch brand, The King's Ginger Liqueur, is a good one to try.

GINGER WINE A grape-based wine flavoured with ginger, plus some other spices and herbs.

GOLDSCHLAGER A strong, cinnamon-flavoured Swiss liqueur containing 24-carat gold flakes.

GRAND MARNIER A Cognac-based, orange-flavoured French liqueur.

GRENADINE A sweet, red non-alcoholic syrup, originally made from pomegranates but now often artificially flavoured.

JACK DANIEL'S See 'Whisky'.

KAHLÚA A dark brown, coffee-flavoured Mexican liqueur.

KUMMEL A colourless Danish liqueur flavoured with caraway seeds and cumin.

LAYERING A cocktail-making technique, which involves carefully pouring liqueurs of different densities on top of each other in a small narrow glass to make an attractive, multi-layered beverage like the B52 or a Pousse Café.

LIQUEUR Known as cordials in the USA, liqueurs are high-quality sweet spirits flavoured with the fruits, seeds, leaves or flowers of plants and often prettily coloured.

MANZANA VERDE A green liqueur with the taste of raw green apples.

MARASCHINO A non-alcoholic syrup flavoured with cherries.

MARASCHINO LIQUEUR A sweet colourless liqueur made from maraska cherries.

MEZCAL Unlike tequila, the production of which is strictly regulated, mezcal is distilled only once and can be made from any agave plant and in any region of Mexico. A bottle of mezcal often has a worm in the bottom.

MIDORI A bright green Japanese liqueur made from musk melons.

MUDDLING A cocktail-making technique, which involves using a barspoon or muddler to mash ingredients such as fruit and herbs in the bottom of a glass so as to release their flavour.

ON THE ROCKS Description of a drink that is served over ice, as opposed to 'straight up', which means served without ice.

ORANGE FLOWER WATER A flavouring made from orange blossom, used in cooking as well as in cocktails.

ORGEAT A milky non-alcoholic syrup flavoured with almonds.

OVERPROOF A description for very strong spirits with an ABV above the average of 40%.

PARFAIT AMOUR A purple-coloured, scented liqueur, made from brandy, oranges, lemons and herbs.

PERNOD A French anise-flavoured spirit, which turns a cloudy pale yellow when mixed with water.

PIMM'S NO. 1 The first of six different spirit-based Pimm's (only two of which are available today), this one is made from gin blended with herb extracts and quinine and was invented in London in 1840 by James Pimm.

PISCO A colourless South American spirit, distilled from the muscat grape and produced in Peru and Chile.

POIRE WILLIAM A pear-flavoured fruit brandy (see 'Brandy'). Liqueur de Poire William is less fiery than the Poire William eau de vie.

PORT A fortified wine made in the same way as sherry and available in several styles, for example tawny, ruby, vintage and white. Originally made only in Portugal, port is now produced in countries such as Australia, America and South Africa.

POUSSE CAFÉ A dramatic-looking cocktail in which various liqueurs of different densities are layered in a small narrow glass.

ROSE WATER A flavouring made from rose petals, used in cooking as well as in cocktails.

RUM A spirit distilled from molasses or directly from the fermented juices of sugar cane. There are hundreds of different rums, ranging in hue from light/white (colourless) through golden colours to dark brown. The majority of rums are produced in the Caribbean.

RYE See 'Whisky'.

SAKE A Japanese alcoholic drink, usually referred to as 'rice wine'.

SAMBUCA A dry, anise-based Italian liqueur flavoured with elderberries. Black sambuca is a thicker and stronger tasting version.

SCHNAPPS A strong distilled colourless spirit, available plain or flavoured, for example apple, butterscotch, cherry, peach, peppermint and strawberry.

SHAKING A cocktail-making technique for thick ingredients that need thorough mixing, which involves combining ingredients together in a cocktail shaker.

SHERRY A fortified wine, available as dry (fino), medium and sweet (oloroso). Sherry was originally made only in the Jérez region of Spain, but is now produced in other regions of Spain and elsewhere in the world, for example the USA and South Africa.

SHOOTER A drink that is served in a shot glass and downed in one.

SLOE GIN A deep red/purple liqueur made from gin flavoured with sugar and sloes.

SOUTHERN COMFORT An American liqueur combining bourbon whiskey with peaches, oranges and herbs, created in New Orleans in the 1880s.

STIRRING A cocktail-making technique for clear drinks, which involves simply mixing the ingredients together in a mixing glass using a barspoon.

STREGA A yellow Italian liqueur with a citrus base and flavoured with herbs.

SUGAR SYRUP Also known as gomme syrup and sirop de gomme, this non-alcoholic syrup made from sugar is available commercially or can be made at home (see page 32).

TEQUILA A Mexican spirit, distilled from the juice of the blue agave plant, one of 400 species of agave, and produced only in certain regions of Mexico. There are four varieties: silver, gold, rested and aged.

TIA MARIA A rum-based, coffee-flavoured Jamaican liqueur.

TRIPLE SEC A colourless orange-flavoured liqueur similar to Cointreau.

VERMOUTH A fortified wine made in both Italy and France, flavoured with herbs, sugar and caramel and available in sweet, dry, red and white versions. Kina Lillet, now known simply as Lillet, and Noilly Prat are highly regarded French vermouths. Cinzano and Martini & Rossi are well-known Italian brands.

VODKA Traditionally perceived as a colourless, tasteless and odourless grain spirit in the West, vodka is also available flavoured. Popular flavourings include bison grass (Zubrowka), blackcurrant, honey, lemon, lime, mandarin, melon, orange peel, pepper and raspberry. Vodka produced in the East yields more flavoursome results.

WHISKY (Scotch/Canadian) or whiskey (US/Irish) A spirit distilled from grain, malt, sugar and yeast, first made in Scotland and Ireland more than 500 years ago. The various Scotch, Irish, Canadian and American whiskies are very different. Scotch whisky is either a single malt or a blend of malt and grain whiskies – mixtures of the same whisky from different years or of different types of whiskies. Irish whiskey is made with a mixture of malted and unmalted barleys and is less pungent than Scotch because the barley is dried in a different type of kiln. All Canadian whisky is blended rye whisky, of a uniform high quality and rather light in both colour and taste. Originally only from Bourbon County, Kentucky, USA, bourbon whiskey is made from at least 51 per cent corn and a blend of barley and rye or wheat, while American rye whiskey is made with at least 51 per cent rye. Jack Daniel's is a 'sour mash' whiskey produced at the Jack Daniel's distillery in Lynchburg, Tennessee, USA.

INDEX

A

Absinthe Cocktail, 87
Alabama Slammer, 148
Amaretto: Blueberry
    Amaretto Sour, 134
  Godchild, 164
  Orange Brûlée, 165
Americano, 145
Añejo Manhattan, 90
aperitifs, 80–7
apple juice: Polish Martini, 66
apples: Apple Manhattan, 91
  Applejack Martini, 67
  Liver Recovery, 173
apricot brandy: Apricot
    Royale, 134
  Mai Tai, 12, 35, 141
Armagnac, 29
Azure Martini, 67

B

B50 Who, 152
B52, 152
Bacardi Cocktail, 87
Bailey's: B50 Who, 152
  B52, 152
  Brain Haemorrhage, 153
  Mudslide, 161
balancing flavours, 30–3
Banana Colada, Virgin, 180
Basil and Honey Fresca, 127
beer: Lagerita, 122
  Submarine, 151
Bellini, 104
berries: Berry Margarita, 99
  Black Bird, 120
  Red Berry Smoothie, 179
Bitter Cosmopolitan, 78
bitter lemon: St Clement's, 178
Black Bird, 120
Black Bison, 70
Black Dog, 73

Black Russian, 159
Black Velvet, 108
blending, 45
Blood and Sand, 164
Blood Martini, 68
Bloody Mary, 173
Blue Blazer, 160
Blueberry Amaretto Sour, 134
Boston Sour, 132
bourbon: Boston Sour, 132
  Horse's Neck, 139
  Mint Julep, 119
  New Orleans Sazarac, 83
  Old-Fashioned, 162
Brain Haemorrhage, 153
brandy, 29
  Brandy Alexander, 29, 163
  Champagne Cocktail, 104
  Corpse Reviver, 174
  Mezcal Margarita, 96
  Sidecar, 29, 32, 86
  Stinger, 29, 163
Brazilian Mule, 138
Breakfast Martini, 68
building, 42

C

cachaça: Azure Martini, 67
  Caipirinha, 118
  Passion Fruit Batida, 123
Caipirinha, 118
Cajun Martini, 75
Calvados, 29
  Apple Manhattan, 91
  Applejack Martini, 67
  Corpse Reviver, 174
Campari: Americano, 145
  Blood Martini, 68
  Negroni, 83
  Sour Italian, 132
canella liqueur: Azure
    Martini, 67
Chambord: Black Bison, 70
  Purple Haze, 154
  Red Cactus, 101

Tres Compadres, 98
champagne, 102–9
  Champagne Cobbler, 121
  Champagne Cocktail, 104
  Champagne Julep, 106
  Royal Gin Fizz, 114
  Tequila Slammer, 150
cherry brandy: Blood and
    Sand, 164
Cherry Martini, 63
chillies: Cajun Martini, 75
Churchill Martini, 56
Citrus Martini, 65
Claret Cobbler, 121
Classic Cosmopolitan, 76
Classic Margarita, 94
Classic Martini, 35, 55
cobblers, 121
coconut cream: Piña
    Colada, 12, 166
  Tequila Colada, 167
  Virgin Banana Colada, 180
coffee: Brazilian Mule, 138
  Irish Coffee, 161
  Vodka Espresso, 158
Cognac, 29
Cointreau: Citrus Martini, 65
  Horny Toad, 95
  Lemon Drop, 154
  Raspberry Torte, 101
  Sidecar, 29, 32, 86
  Strawberry Cosmopolitan, 79
  Tres Compadres, 98
collinses, 110, 112–13
Conmemorativo, 122
coolers, 136–45
Corpse Reviver, 174
Cosmo Royale, 79
cosmopolitans, 76–9
Cowboy Hoof, 119
cranberry juice: Blood
    Martini, 68
  cosmopolitans, 76–9
  cranberry cooler, 178

Detox, 152
  Jamaican Breeze, 142
  Madras, 140
  Pontberry Martini, 68
  Sea Breeze, 141
  Tropical Breeze, 140
creamy cocktails, 156–69
crème de cacao: Brandy
    Alexander, 29, 163
  Golden Cadillac, 168
  Hazelnut Martini, 70
  Silk Stocking, 166
  Turkish Chocolate, 71
crème de cassis: Kir Royale,
    107
crème de fraise de bois:
    Strawberry Mule, 138
crème de framboise: Claret
    Cobbler, 121
  Metropolis, 108
crème de menthe:
    Grasshopper, 168
  Stinger, 29, 163
  Vodka Stinger, 175
crème de mure: Gin
    Bramble, 128
  Legend, 68
crème de pêche: Bellini, 104
Cuba Libre, 128
curaçao: Mai Tai, 12, 35, 141

D

daiquiris, 32, 84–5
Dark and Stormy, 128
Detox, 152
digestifs, 156–69
Drambuie: Rusty Nail, 160
Dry Manhattan, 89

E

Elderflower Collins, 113
equipment, 37–9

F

FDR Martini, 60
Fernet Branca: Stormy
    Weather, 175

fixes, 124–9
fizzes, 110, 114–15
flaming, 35, 45
flavours, balancing, 30–3
French Martini, 65
French 75, 109
Fresca, 126–7
frostings, 35

G

Galliano: Harvey
    Wallbanger, 145
  Sour Italian, 132
garnishes, 35, 48
Gazpacho, 172
Gibson, 57
gin, 20–1
  Cowboy Hoof, 119
  Elderflower Collins, 113
  fizzes, 114–15
  French 75, 109
  Gin Bramble, 128
  Gin Gimlet, 20, 83
  Golden Bronx, 169
  martinis, 55–60, 72
  Negroni, 83
  Pink Gin, 82
  Red Snapper, 172
  Silver Bronx, 169
  Sloe Gin Fizz, 115
ginger beer: Dark and
    Stormy, 128
  Horse's Neck, 139
  Moscow Mule, 138
  Pimm's Cup, 139
Ginger Champagne, 105
Ginger Cosmopolitan, 76
ginger liqueur: Horse's, 59
ginger wine: Brazilian Mule,
    138
glasses, 40–1, 47
  chilling, 69
  frosting, 35
Godchild, 164
Golden Bronx, 169

Golden Cadillac, 168
Goldschlager: Triple Gold
    Margarita, 94
Gotham, 73
Grand Marnier: B52, 152
    Orange Brûlée, 165
grapefruit juice: Hemingway
    Daiquiri, 85
    Pussy Foot, 183
    Salty Mexican Dog, 144
    Sea Breeze, 141
    Tropical Breeze, 140
Grasshopper, 168
Green Iguana, 96
grenadine: Shirley Temple,
    182
Guinness: Black Velvet, 108

H
hangover cures, 170–3
Harvey Wallbanger, 145
Hazelnut Martini, 70
Hemingway Daiquiri, 85
Herba Buena, 26, 96
Hibiscus Martini, 123
highballs, 136–45
history of cocktails, 8–12
Honey Colada, 166
Horny Toad, 95
Horse's, 59
Horse's Neck, 139
Hot Toddy, 162

I
ice, 39, 47–8, 69
Iced Tea, 181
ingredients, 17
Irish whiskey, 23
    Irish Coffee, 161

J
Jack Daniels, 23
    Lynchburg Lemonade, 23,
    129
Jamaican Breeze, 142
James Bond, 109
Joe Average, 74

juices, 17

K
Kahlúa: B50 Who, 152
    B52, 152
    Black Russian, 159
    Mudslide, 161
    White Russian, 159
Kamikaze, 148
Kina Lillet: Vesper, 58
Kir Royale, 107
Knob Creek: Premium
    Manhattan, 90
Krupnik Sour, 132
kummel: Silver Streak, 158

L
Lagerita, 122
layering, 42
Legend, 68
lemon juice, 32
    Citrus Martini, 65
    collinses, 112–13
    fizzes, 114–15
    French 75, 109
    Hot Toddy, 162
    Lemon Drop, 154
    Lemon Meringue, 165
    Orange Daiquiri, 84
    sours, 132–5
lemonade: Lynchburg
    Lemonade, 23, 129
    Old-Fashioned Lemonade,
    183
    Pimm's Cup, 139
    Shirley Temple, 182
lemons, garnishes, 35
lime cordial: Gin Gimlet, 20,
    83
lime juice, 32
    Bacardi Cocktail, 87
    cosmopolitans, 78–9
    daiquiris, 84–5
    Gin Bramble, 128
    Horny Toad, 95
    Legend, 68

rickeys, 96, 113
limes, garnishes, 35
liqueurs, 17, 29, 32
Liquorice Martini, 71
Liver Recovery, 173
Los Tres Amigos, 151
Lynchburg Lemonade, 23,
    129

M
Madras, 140
Mai Tai, 12, 35, 141
Mangorita, 100
Manhattans, 23, 88–91
Manzana Verde: Applejack
    Martini, 67
margaritas, 32, 92–101
Martinez, 59
martinis, 10–11, 52–75, 123
measures, 37
Metropolis, 108
Metropolitan, 78
mezcal, 26
    Mezcal Margarita, 96
Midori: Green Iguana, 96
    Midori Sour, 135
Mimosa, 106
mint: Champagne Julep, 106
    Cowboy Hoof, 119
    Mint Julep, 119
    Mojito, 119
mixers, 17, 48
mocktails, 176–83
Mojito, 119
Montgomery, 57
Moscow Mule, 138
muddling, 44
Mudslide, 161
Mulato Daiquiri, 85
mules, 138

N
Naked Martini, 56
Negroni, 83
New Orleans Fizz, 114
New Orleans Sazarac, 83

O
Old-Fashioned, 162
Old-Fashioned Lemonade,
    183
olive brine: FDR Martini, 60
Orange and Pear Fresca, 127
Orange Brûlée, 165
Orange Daiquiri, 84
orange juice: Alabama
    Slammer, 148
    Golden Bronx, 169
    Golden Cadillac, 168
    Madras, 140
    Mimosa, 106
    Planter's Punch, 142
    Pussy Foot, 183
    St Clement's, 178
    Silver Bronx, 169
    Tequila Sunrise, 12, 144
oranges, garnishes, 35
Original Daiquiri, 84

P
Passion Fruit Batida, 123
peaches: Bellini, 104
    Peach Rickey, 113
Pear Martini, 65
Perfect Manhattan, 89
Pernod: New Orleans
    Sazarac, 83
Personaltini, 61
Pimm's Cup, 139
Pinarita, 100
pineapple juice: French
    Martini, 65
    Jamaican Breeze, 142
    Piña Colada, 12, 166
    Pinarita, 100
    Rum Runner, 142
    Tequila Colada, 167
    Virgin Banana Colada, 180
Pink Gin, 82
Pisco Sour, 135
Planter's Punch, 142
Polish Martini, 66
Pomegranate, 63
Pontberry Martini, 68
port, 29
    Port and Blackberry
        Fresca, 127
    Port Cobbler, 121
Pousse Café, 42, 149
Prairie Oyster, 174
Premium Manhattan, 90
Prickly Pear Margarita, 99
Prohibition, 10, 12
punches, 136–45
Purple Haze, 154
Pussy Foot, 183
R
raspberries: Raspberry
        Martini, 62
    Raspberry Rickey, 112
    Raspberry Torte, 101
    Red Cactus, 101
    Rossini, 106

Red Berry Smoothie, 179
Red Cactus, 101
Red Snapper, 172
Red Star, 74
rickeys, 110, 112
Rob Roy, 23, 91
rose water: New Orleans
    Fizz, 114
Rossini, 106
Royal Gin Fizz, 114
Rude Cosmopolitan, 76
rum, 24–5
    Bacardi Cocktail, 87
    Black Dog, 73
    Cuba Libre, 128
    daiquiris, 84–5
    Dark and Stormy, 128
    Honey Colada, 166
    Jamaican Breeze, 142
    Mai Tai, 12, 35, 141
    Mojito, 119
    Piña Colada, 12, 166
    Planter's Punch, 142
    Rum Runner, 142
    T-Punch, 142
Rusty Nail, 160
rye whiskey, 23
    Manhattans, 23, 89
S
St Clement's, 178
Sake Martini, 66
Salty Mexican Dog, 144
Sangrita, 154
Sapphire Martini, 72
schnapps: Brain
        Haemorrhage, 153
    Brazilian Mule, 138
    Detox, 152
Scorpion, 12
Screwdriver, 30
Sea Breeze, 141
serving cocktails, 47–8
shakers, 37–8
shaking, 44–5

sherry, 29
Shirley Temple, 182
shooters, 146–55
Sidecar, 29, 32, 86
Silk Stocking, 166
Silver Bronx, 169
Silver Streak, 158
sippers, 146–55
slammers, 146–55
sloe gin: Alabama
        Slammer, 148
    Sloe Gin Fizz, 115
smashes, 116–23
souring agents, 30–3
sours, 130–5
Southern Comfort: Alabama
        Slammer, 148
spirits, 17, 18–27
St Clement's, 178
Stinger, 29, 163
stirring, 44
Stormy Weather, 175
strawberries: Strawberry
        Cosmopolitan, 79
    Strawberry Martini, 63
    Strawberry Mule, 138
Strega: Sour Italian, 132
Submarine, 151
sugar syrup, 32, 33
Sweet Manhattan, 89
sweetness, balancing
        flavours, 30–3
T
T-Punch, 142
Tea, Iced, 181
techniques, 42–5
tequila, 26–7
    Añejo Manhattan, 90
    Conmemorativo, 122
    Lagerita, 122
    margaritas, 92–101
    Salty Mexican Dog, 144
    Sangrita, 154
    Silk Stocking, 166

Submarine, 151
Tequila Colada, 167
Tequila Rickey, 96
Tequila Slammer, 150
Tequila Sunrise, 12, 144
Tequilini, 75
    Los Tres Amigos, 151
Thunderer, 73
tomato juice: Bloody Mary,
        173
    Red Snapper, 172
    Virgin Mary, 182
Los Tres Amigos, 151
Tres Compadres, 98
Triple Gold Margarita, 94
triple sec: cosmopolitans,
        76–8
    margaritas, 94, 96, 99–101
Tropical Breeze, 140
Turkish Chocolate, 71
U
Ultimate Martini, 60
V
vermouth, 29
    Americano, 145
    Blood and Sand, 164
    Corpse Reviver, 174
    Manhattans, 89–91
    martinis, 55–60, 74–5
    Negroni, 83
    Red Star, 74
    Stormy Weather, 175
    Tequilini, 75
Vesper, 58
Virgin Banana Colada, 180
Virgin Mary, 182
Virgin Mojito, 181
vodka, 18–19
    Alabama Slammer, 148
    Black Bird, 120
    Black Russian, 159
    Bloody Mary, 173
    Claret Cobbler, 121
    cosmopolitans, 76, 78–9

Detox, 152
Fresca, 126–7
Gazpacho, 172
Ginger Champagne, 105
Godchild, 164
Harvey Wallbanger, 145
James Bond, 109
Kamikaze, 148
Krupnik Sour, 132
Lemon Drop, 154
Lemon Meringue, 165
Madras, 140
martinis, 55, 57–71,
        73–5, 123
Metropolis, 108
Mudslide, 161
mules, 138
Peach Rickey, 113
Purple Haze, 154
Raspberry Rickey, 112
Sea Breeze, 141
Silver Streak, 158
Tropical Breeze, 140
Vodka Collins, 18, 112
Vodka Espresso, 158
Vodka Stinger, 175
White Russian, 159
W
whiskey see bourbon; Irish
        whiskey; rye whiskey
whisky, 23
    Blood and Sand, 164
    Blue Blazer, 160
    Hot Toddy, 162
    Rob Roy, 23, 91
    Rusty Nail, 160
    Smoky Martini, 55
    White Russian, 159
wines, fortified, 29
Y
yoghurt: Red Berry
        Smoothie, 179
Z
zests, 35

ACKNOWLEDGMENTS

This book, more than any other, has been an intensive lesson in teamwork! And for that thanks must be given to many. First, all at RPS. Notably Alison for giving me the opportunity to continue to promote the world of cocktails, Catherine for adding a touch of style to the photo-shoot, carried out whilst pregnant – all those cocktails going to waste!! But mostly to Miriam, without whose motivation I'd probably have found it difficult to get out of bed most mornings.
Thanks to Messrs Altman and Turner at IPBartenders for their knowledge, patience and general banter (although there's nothing clever or grown up about drinking Aperol.)
William Lingwood has excelled himself once again in bringing the drinks to life (even the brown ones!) his pictures tell their own story.

PICTURE CREDITS

All commissioned photography by William Lingwood

Page 8, image courtesy of Vin Mag Archive; page 10 image courtesy of Topham Picturepoint; pages 11 & 12 images courtesy of The Advertising Archive; page 13 image courtesy of Topham/HIP